Alastair Robertson has been keenly interested in local history for many years, and has written many articles and several books in that vein.

Parallel to this has been an interest in world history, in particular Spain and the island of Tenerife, about the history of which he has written over 100 articles that have been translated into Spanish for publication on the island. This is his first book concerning national and international history.

To the memory of Don Antonio

Alastair Robertson

1589 – THE ENGLISH ARMADA AND THE FORTUNES OF DON ANTONIO

Austin Macauley Publishers™

LONDON * CAMBRIDGE * NEW YORK * SHARJAH

Copyright © Alastair Robertson 2024

The right of Alastair Robertson to be identified as author of this work has been asserted by the author in accordance with sections 77 and 78 of the Copyright, Designs and Patents Act 1988.

All rights reserved. No part of this publication may be reproduced, stored in a retrieval system, or transmitted in any form or by any means, electronic, mechanical, photocopying, recording, or otherwise, without the prior permission of the publishers.

Any person who commits any unauthorised act in relation to this publication may be liable to criminal prosecution and civil claims for damages.

The story, experiences, and words are the author's alone.

A CIP catalogue record for this title is available from the British Library.

ISBN 9781035855742 (Paperback)
ISBN 9781035855759 (ePub e-book)

www.austinmacauley.com

First Published 2024
Austin Macauley Publishers Ltd®
1 Canada Square
Canary Wharf
London
E14 5AA

Austin Macauley publishers

Introduction

In the spring of 1589 a fleet of 125 English ships with 23,000 men on board was ready to leave port. It had three specific instructions from Queen Elizabeth, 1) to destroy all warships in Spanish and Portuguese ports, 2) to take the islands of the Azores for England, and 3) to set on throne of Portugal Don Antonio, Prior of Crato, a man of royal Portuguese blood, an act which would at once regain independence for the country from Spain and gain an indebted ally on Spain's doorstep. Holland was to send ships and men, the Sultan of Turkey, to whom England was supplying war materiel, promised to send his navy to harass the Spanish coast, the Shereef of Morocco was to supply troops, and the king and queen mother of France were in full support.

Spain was to be surrounded by hostile forces. Sir John Norris, a battle-hardened veteran of the English army in the Low Countries, commanded the land troops, and Sir Francis Drake, the nation's hero, was in command of the fleet. Everything looked set to deliver a body blow to King Philip and Spain. On the 28th of April the fleet set sail.

The English Armada, or the Lisbon Expedition as it is more usually and quite dismissively referred to, is mentioned in a sentence, or a paragraph, or a short chapter in most histories, and yet it was as significantly disastrous to England as the Invincible Armada was to Spain. The world knows about the Spanish Armada, but hardly anyone has heard of the English attempt at revenge.

However, the seeds for the Enterprise of Lisbon, the English Armada, had been sown eleven years before, in Morocco. Throughout the intervening years one man was at times central and at times peripheral to the international events, Don Antonio, Prior of Crato who throughout the 1580s was alternately celebrated and shunned by the rulers of England and France.

Tensions between England and Spain increased all through the reign of Queen Elizabeth. English ships persistently raided Spanish shipping and English soldiers supported their Protestant colleagues in the Low Countries. Spain at the time was at its peak of expansion that had culminated with the absorption of

Portugal in 1580 and King Philip II was permanently annoyed and frustrated by this "queen of half an island," as he referred to Elizabeth.

Throckmorton's Plot of 1583, an attack "by all the Catholic powers" to include the assassination of Elizabeth, was foiled by the spies of Sir Francis Walsingham. Bernardino Mendoza, the Spanish ambassador and spymaster to London, was dismissed in January the following year.

When the Duke of Guise raised an army in France and Philip prepared an army in the Spanish Netherlands, Elizabeth was ready for open war and her aid to Low Countries began.

In 1586 the Babington Plot was foiled by Walsingham, to be followed by the execution on 8th February 1587 of Mary Queen of Scots, and event that shocked Europe and hastened the plans of King Philip of Spain, the world champion of Catholicism, to invade and conquer England. But in 1587 Drake's raid on Cadiz delayed the intended Invincible Armada.

Drake's expedition in 1587 to Cadiz to "singe the king of Spain's beard," that prevented the Spanish fleet from assembling, and his Great Caribbean raid of 1586 are both famous historical events in English history, but they had both been assembled for a completely different purpose. In both cases the original intention had been to serve Don Antonio, King Antony, in his attempts to gain the throne of Portugal.

The aim of this book is to shed light for the reader with a general interest in history on a little-known and misinterpreted episode in this dramatic period of Queen Elizabeth's reign. To impart an atmosphere of events as they happened the references used are all, as nearly as possibly, contemporary documents, the various Calendars of State Papers and the diary of Wingfield, or Pricket. The reports by the anonymous Venetian ambassador to the Doge seem a particularly impartial record. So as not to be influenced by interpretations of historians, the author has kept references from other sources to an absolute minimum.

The account written by Captain Anthony Wingfield, or Robert Pricket, the identity of the author is uncertain, and referred to in this text as Wingfield/Pricket, is vivid and immediate, it has been occasionally edited, paraphrased or quoted directly, but used by this author to the extent that he deserves to be named as co-author for a large part of the second section of the narrative.

Alastair Robertson
June 2024

Don Antonio, Prior of Crato, the man who would be King of Portugal

Part One –
The Path To 1589

1578 – 1579

THE DEATH OF KING SEBASTIAN I AND THE QUESTION OF THE PORTUGUESE SUCCESSION

1578

The appearance of Don Antonio, Prior of Crato, on the international stage began when the succession to the throne of Portugal was cast into doubt in 1578. In that year the impetuous young Portuguese king, Sebastian I, embarked on what he saw as a crusade, only to be killed in battle in northern Morocco aged only twenty-four and childless.

The political situation in northern Morocco in 1578 was that it was made up of four states, the Kingdom of Fez, the Kingdom of Marrakesh, the Kingdom of Sus, and the Kingdom of Tafilalet. The Kingdom of Fez was often in a state of turmoil, with fratricide being a frequent occurrence.

Some years before 1578, the governor of Morocco, Muley Abdallah al-Galiband, with his son, Abdallah Mahomet, surnamed the Negro because his mother was a negress, had plotted and carried out the murder of his brother and former governor, Muley Abdulmomen of Tremecen. When Muley Abdallah died in 1574 his son succeeded as Muley Abu Abdallah Mahomet II.

Like his father Muley Mahomet was cruel man, having killed, to secure his position, two of his brothers and imprisoned a third. He was hated by his subjects, until Muley Abd al-Malik, a younger brother of Muley Abdallah, in a popular move, with Ottoman support instigated a successful revolt to overthrow his nephew to become the new King of Morocco. Muley Mahomet, as the deposed ruler, then went to Portugal to request the help of King Sebastian, who was already assembling an army for a crusade in Africa.

Once in Africa, the combined army of King Sebastian of Portugal and Abu Abdallah Mahomet II met the opposing force of a large army under Muley Abd al-Malik. The ensuing Battle of Alcacer Quibir, also known as the Battle of Ksar el-Kebir, and the Battle of the Three Kings, was fought on 4th August 1578. King Sebastian was killed and Muley Mahomet, who was serving in his army, drowned while crossing a river. Muley Abd al-Malik, who was seriously ill before the battle, died at the moment of victory leaving his younger brother, Muley Ahmad al-Mansur, to finish and win the battle, after which he was proclaimed King, or Shereef, of Morocco.

The Battle of the Three Kings, 4th August 1578

Muley Ahmad al-Mansur proved to be a popular king up to his death in 1603. He was acutely aware of the international scene, and to ensure good relations with his powerful neighbour, King Philip II of Spain, he sent the body of King Sebastian back to Portugal for re-burial at Philip's request, but this event notwithstanding, he was to be a potential ally of England and Don Antonio in the events of 1589.

In the meantime, because King Sebastian had died without taken the precaution of producing an heir to succeed him before he left on his escapade, his nearest male relative in the Portuguese royal house of Aziz, was his sixty-six year old uncle, Cardinal Henry, who had taken a vow of chastity, and who now ascended the throne as King Henry I of Portugal.

On the indirect line of succession after Cardinal King Henry there were five claimants to the crown descended from King Manuel I, the great-grandfather of Sebastian. The line of Manuel's eldest son, King John III, was now extinct; King Philip II of Spain was a grandson through his mother Isabella, Manuel's eldest daughter; Emmanuel Philbert, Duke of Savoy, was a claimant through his mother Beatrice, Manuel's second daughter; Ranuccio, Duke of Parma, was entitled through his mother Maria, the elder daughter of Manuel's youngest son Duarte; Catherine of Braganza, the youngest daughter of Duarte, was also a claimant with an additional claim through her husband, her first cousin Juan, who was also of the royal House of Braganza; and finally there was Don Antonio, the Prior of Crato, who was the only male heir on the direct line of Manuel by his father Luis, the second son of Manuel. There was only one obstacle in his way – Don Antonio was illegitimate.

1579

The age and the infirmity of Cardinal King Henry made it evident that his reign would not be a long one. With this in mind King Philip began to prepare the way in Spain for his own accession to the crown. For example, a letter dated 2nd August 1579 was sent from Don Manrique de Ayamonte to the town council of Ayamonte, a district of Spain adjacent to the border with south-east Portugal, which stated Philip's case:

He was nearest kin to Cardinal King Henry, his uncle; Don Antonio was illegitimate; Emmanuel Philbert, the Duke of Savoy was younger (although younger only by one year); Catherine, Duchess of Braganza, was a woman; and Ranuccio Farnese was a degree further off. King Philip expressed the advantages to be gained under him by a close connection to Spain.

The Portuguese situation was being closely monitored in England. On 18th August Edward Wooton, the English ambassador to Portugal, sent Queen Elizabeth a report listing the points for and against all the claimants:

He said of Emmanuel Philbert, the Duke of Savoy, and Rannucio, the ten-year old Prince of Parma, "their parts are the least in the pudding." Emmanuel Philbert was soon out of the running in any case because he died the following year.

The Cardinal King Henry did not favour Don Antonio because of his dissolute life. He had fathered many bastards by base women, most of them by New Christians, or converted Moors. By advancing them Don Antonio might threaten the nobility. Wooton wrote that Don Antonio, even though he was the Prior of Crato, was very poor and therefore could not influence the nobility by wealth, nor was he likely to be able to maintain power through them in his favour.

He was, however, well-beloved of the ordinary people, being gracious in his behaviour and liberal with his spending. His advantages were that he was also male and of the direct male royal blood line, although illegitimate. He was, in addition, Portuguese.

About Juan, the 6th Duke of Braganza, joint heir and claimant by marriage to his first cousin, Catherine the daughter of Duarte, King Manuel's youngest son, King Henry favoured him as did many of the nobility, but he was "not beloved of the common people." Nothing was said about the duke's wealth. When Juan died in 1583, his wife Catherine of Braganza became a claimant in her own right, although she had the disadvantage of the time of being female. Interestingly, the House of Braganza had begun with an illegitimate son of King John I, who reigned from 1385 to 1433, who himself was illegitimate.

Finally, there was Philip II, king of Spain. His disadvantages were that his claim was through the female line, and, that he was only half Portuguese. There was also the hatred, great and deep rooted, between Portuguese and Castilians, as the Spanish were generally called, and the resultant international relations with Philip on the throne would not be to Portugal's advantage.

The Portuguese wished to be governed by a king of their own nation, however, whereas Don Antonio had the right, King Philip had the might, which was a distinct advantage, having the power to take the throne by force if need be.

Cardinal King Henry himself had been wrestling with this thorny problem, and one month after Wooton's letter, on 18th September, he issued his decision about Don Antonio's claim to legitimacy and his claim to the succession. He said that Don Antonio had provided no proof of the marriage between his parents, except for a few short statements by interested parties, and that his father, Luis Duke of Beja, had always referred to Don Antonio as his natural son, so, in conclusion, King Henry therefore pronounced Don Antonio to be illegitimate, that the witnesses concerned were accused of giving false statements and were to be arrested.

Don Antonio was greatly alarmed, he protested that he had been given only two days' notice to provide proofs of his claims while the other claimants had been granted more time. He added a lengthy grievance about having been treated unfairly. Even so, his illegitimacy should have been no great obstacle, his ancestor King John I was illegitimate, and the line of his cousins and competitors of the House of Braganza had begun with an illegitimate son of King John. He could have found sympathy in England in Queen Elizabeth, who had been declared illegitimate by her own father, Henry VIII, when he had annulled his marriage to her mother, Ann Boleyn.

Although Elizabeth's illegitimacy was regarded in many circles as a technicality, nevertheless it was only by an Act of Parliament in 1544 that she was legitimised, while in the Catholic world she was still regarded as illegitimate. So there were precedents for overcoming illegitimacy – where there was a will. There is also a possibility, a suspicion only, that if Cardinal King Henry had acknowledged Don Antonio as a legitimate heir to the throne, then Henry himself would have been a usurper.

1580
King Antonio

When Cardinal King Henry's imminent death became apparent, a regency council of five governors were appointed to decide the claims to succession of the Portuguese crown. Of the two native-born Portuguese claimants, Catherine, Duchess of Braganza, and through her, her husband Juan, Duke of Braganza, was timid and unprepared, while the other, Don Antonio, was ambitious, bold and eager. It was to him that all who were patriotic grouped themselves. The poorer classes bitterly hated foreigners, particularly Spaniards and their King Philip, who was really the only other serious claimant.

King Philip II of Spain

Cardinal King Henry I died on 31st January 1580, aged 68. By his will the whole issue should be decided by the course of justice. The five governors of Portugal sent word to the European heads of state that they had taken charge of government.

With the Portuguese succession in doubt, in England the ever-practical Elizabeth was hesitant about making trade agreements between the two countries pending a resolution. Initial thoughts were that if Philip was to succeed to the throne with Portuguese acceptance then better trade might result. And as well as European observers monitoring the situation, from across the Straits of Gibraltar Ahmad al-Mansur, the shereef of Morocco, saw Don Antonio as a potential ally against Spain and he was ready to meet him.

The late king had decided in favour of Philip, and the Portuguese nobles and higher clergy felt inclined to agree, although it was acknowledged that the mass of the people were against him and that a small amount of force might be necessary to help him acquire the throne.

With Don Antonio being referred to as unlawful or a bastard, he appeared to be out of contention, but straight after Cardinal King Henry's death Don Antonio obtained a Bull from the Pope stating that his cause should be heard by a papal nuncio and the Bishop of Lisbon. As a Portuguese claimant of royal blood he had the support of the people, and the lower churchmen of the country were devotedly attached to him, because, as Prior of Crato, he was also an ecclesiastical claimant. Then there was the belief, a mistaken belief as it turned out, that the nobility were Portuguese above everything, and so Don Antonio was proclaimed King of Portugal.

It was obvious that this situation would be unacceptable to King Philip. For two years he had intrigued, suborned, bribed and threatened leading Portuguese nobles and the higher clergy to acknowledge his right to the succession, pointing out the advantages to them if he were to be chosen. He was ready and indeed he was expecting to accede to the throne, but diplomatically he had awaited developments. Militarily of course he was infinitely stronger than Don Antonio, which was a factor that could well deter France or England from interfering by direct action.

There was resentment and open opposition to Philip from Portuguese nationalists. The Bishop of Guarda declared that Don Antonio was the only legitimate heir and raised an army of the people to resist any attempt by King

Philip to take the crown by force. But Philip had prepared for this and a Spanish army was already on the border with Portugal.

Philip assumed he would become king of Portugal but the five governors were not to be rushed. The Duchess of Braganza and Don Antonio had papal Bulls to be considered, and an observer noted that, "The whole country is marvellously inclined to Don Antonio." As a precaution against any unrest and interference the governors levied 1,000 foot and 600 horse for their defence.

By March progress towards the appointment of a new king was taking shape. To pave the way for himself, King Philip sent a request to Don Antonio asking for his allegiance, acknowledging that if he did so then all of Portugal would follow.

In April Don Antonio wrote to Catherine de Medici, the Queen Mother of Henry III of France, who was to prove to be his staunchest supporter, confessing that he was not hopeful. King Philip had gained control over the chief men and the five governors, who he hoped were favouring him, but the people of Portugal were preparing to defend themselves, with the confidence of help from France. Philip was hoping to frighten the Portuguese into submission but they assured Don Antonio that they were not alarmed.

Don Antonio, in the meantime, was still seeking to be recognised as the rightful claimant by a revocation of King Henry's pronouncement; he had received written support from the Pope for quashing the decision made by Henry.

The Portuguese ambassador in France appealed to Queen Elizabeth for support, reminding her of Portugal's support for her in the past, for she too had once been proclaimed illegitimate, and that Philip was now regarded as a usurper; but there was suspicion that the letter had been strongly influenced by the French monarchy. Elizabeth also received a letter from the governors who assured her that they would give the crown to the rightful heir, whoever it should be, and if imposed upon, they cautioned her, they would defend themselves. In May, Catherine, Duchess of Braganza, urged Elizabeth to support the rightful claimant but gave no name. Perhaps it was a subtle plea for Elizabeth's support in her own claim. She informed Elizabeth that if she could not get justice for herself, she would obey the appointed king, whoever it might be.

King Philip, concerned by Don Antonio's popularity and wishing for a peaceful accession, tried to buy him off by promising him the prestigious Priorate of Castile if he relinquished his claim. The governors were doing their best to be even-handed, they were in communication with King Philip, requesting his assurance that he would not use force, for this would negate his claim to the crown. Otherwise, they were in doubt as to who had strongest claim between Don Antonio and the Duchess of Braganza. Then, as if to add to Portugal's troubles, a plague broke out in Lisbon.

By June a civil war was looming, Don Antonio's case was strengthened when he re-stated his right to the crown by virtue of the Bull from the Pope. The bearer of a letter from Don Antonio to Queen Elizabeth was authorised to speak in his name, he carried proofs of Don Antonio's legitimacy, and he called upon the English to give their help in consideration of the good understanding between their two countries. He declared that Don Antonio was favoured by the Portuguese people and that they were ready to resist Spanish intervention, but they needed aid in the form of munitions.

English aid was to have been facilitated by Secretary Wilson, to whom Don Antonio had sent a bezoar stone worth fifty crowns from the Portuguese crown jewels which he had secured for himself. Bezoar stones were rare, they came from the stomach of certain animals and were believed to have mystical healing properties. But Elizabeth, as was her wont, prevaricated for so long that Don Antonio's representative went instead to Antwerp for help.

This attempted act of collusion annoyed Bernardino de Mendoza, the Spanish Ambassador and Philip's spy master at the French court, who considered objecting to Queen Elizabeth if such an alliance had resulted. However, he wrote reassuringly to King Philip that the English knew Don Antonio had no right to the throne and that whatever was said on his behalf was all lies.

Practical support in France for Don Antonio's cause was seen to be a reality when a French ship with a cargo of munitions, believed to be bound for Portugal, was detained at Plymouth, but it was allowed to continue on its way. Moral support was cheaper and Elizabeth, playing the *agent provocateur*, encouraged the divisions in Portugal, she was in favour of anything that annoyed Spain so she sent a letter of encouragement to Don Antonio. A Portuguese, Juan Rodriguez de Souza, a Knight of the Order of Christ, arrived in England with letters that Mendoza suspected were from Don Antonio, who had been "in loving converse" with some Englishmen who supported him. But there was no apparent reaction from Elizabeth. Mendoza put it about that it was believed that the quality of Don Antonio's messenger did not impress Elizabeth or the court, that he was only a common servant.

However, to muddy the waters still further, Elizabeth's spymaster and chief intriguer, Sir Francis Walsingham, sent out a false report that English arms and men were being sent to Bayonne and onwards with the purpose to support Portugal.

Perhaps unsurprisingly, the five governors chose the least controversial but weakest candidate, who was the candidate least acceptable to anyone else. On 17th June they requested that Juan, Duke of Braganza, take on the government of Portugal. This caused an immediate reaction, on Sunday 19th in the town of Santarem, some forty miles north of Lisbon, where Don Antonio and pope's legate were waiting, after a rousing sermon by the Bishop of Guarda the cry went up for "Don Antonio, King of Portugal!"

As a matter of form, Don Antonio modestly refused to accept the acclaim, stating that he wished only to be head governor and defender of the realm, but nevertheless he was proclaimed king. Next day, the 20th June, the capital city of Lisbon declared for him, however the governors did not accept this, they banned all talk of it and imposed a curfew, while on the border to Spain King Philip was waiting with his forces. Juan, Duke of Braganza, backed off and declared he was ready to do homage to whoever the judges decided should be the successor.

On 23rd Don Antonio travelled from Santarem to Lisbon with 200 horse. Fourteen bands of soldiers were sent against him but they were persuaded to defect, and so he entered the city with people crying for King Antonio. That night, the head officers of the chamber who were in the town of Setubal, across the River Tagus from Lisbon, fled, taking with them money and treasure. Crossing the border, King Philip invaded and took possession of nearby towns. The country people on the road to Lisbon were confused as to who to support for the best.

Elizabeth sent instructions to her envoy in Portugal, first to meet the governors, then in secret to contact Don Antonio, to express hope for his success and giving him a promise of assistance, while publicly she showed hesitation to support any claimant. At first she instructed her agent to advise Don Antonio that if the legal decision went against him he should desist in his claim, but a few days later she encouraged him by saying that he should "attain by the sword what law and right will not give him."

Don Antonio was sworn king in every town on his way to Lisbon, but the governors now were inclined towards Philip. As soon as Don Antonio arrived at gate of Mororia to Lisbon the soldiers turned down their pikes and received him with great joy. He went to main church to give thanks and then to the palace beside the river, and all the time the plague was raging in the city. After four days he went to Setubal to take the town and to arrest the governors, but they had already left by sea. Too late he sent four ships after them. It had been a close call for the governors; they had had to escape from the window of a house in the port.

A guard had then been called out against the governors, calling them traitors, but, disappointingly, a good many noblemen had gone with them. Don Antonio's proclamation as king in Lisbon was reportedly, perhaps by the Spanish, to have been against the will of the nobility, who in the main had been influenced by Philip.

The anonymous Venetian ambassador to the court of Spain made quite an impartial observer, he reported to his master the Doge that King Don Antonio entered Setubal with 8,000 horse and foot where he was also received with great joy and was sworn as king. He then went to the castle in the town. He returned to Lisbon three days later and stayed there with all the remaining nobility. The defences of the River Tagus were strengthened with "a good navy" and it was made sure that the castles were all in good order.

Don Antonio planned that after two more days he would go again to Santarem to make his soldiers ready to resist King Philip. The Venetian ambassador broke with his diplomatic neutrality when he added to his report, "God send him victory for he is a prince worthy to be beloved."

In the Low Countries William of Orange was getting ready to supply arms to Portugal and the Portuguese agent, Giraldo, urged Queen Elizabeth to do the same. By mutual agreement between England and Spain, the situation in Portugal was not to be allowed to affect Spanish shipping in England or English ships in Spanish ports, even though Elizabeth was annoyed by the aid being given to Irish insurgents in Spain. When the Portuguese agent left Antwerp, Bernardino de Mendoza, who was by now the Spanish ambassador in London, was aware that someone was to be sent from England to Portugal, ostensibly bearing letters but in reality a spy.

King Philip had departed from Badajos, just across the Spanish border due east of Lisbon, and entered Portugal on the 27th June, marching towards the capital, sarcastically declaring he was going "to visit the new king, whose reign is not likely to last long." The Portuguese towns of Yelves, Villa, Vicios and Ronces were surrendering to him and the strength of his army. Spanish propaganda put it about that Don Antonio was believed to have no money, no arms, no forces, no captains nor trained soldiers.

Don Antonio sent a representative to Philip's commander, Fernando Alvarez de Toldeo, the Duke of Alva, who refused to speak to him and sent him on to the king. Because of his resistance to the mighty king of Spain, Don Antonio had increased his standing further in the eyes of the people. However, Philip was supposed to have 25,000 men, more than at first had been expected, but the Portuguese ambassador in Madrid did not believe the reports but nevertheless he wanted to send more munitions.

The Duke of Alva was soon close to Setubal and within fifteen or twenty miles of Lisbon where a Spanish fleet was to meet him. The Duke of Medina Sedonia, commander of the fleet, was at Ayamonte, at the mouth of the River Guadiana, which formed the border, and was guarding the coast. An English observer, Roger Bodenham, had little faith in the cause of Don Antonio, he wrote to Secretary Wilson that Don Antonio had been proclaimed king "by a few of the worst sort of people," and about Portugal, "It will be the greatest conquest that ever Spain made since the conquest of the India." The Duke of Alva was thought to be ready to lay siege to Setubal by the 16th, and he expected it to surrender quickly.

The Spanish put stories about that Don Antonio's party was very small, that he had raised base persons to knighthood, that he gave whatever wealth he had very liberally to those around him, that his men in Lisbon were not disposed to fight. Don Antonio himself was reported to be sad and heavy, but this does not ring true, for on Tuesday 12th he went crossed the Tagus with some force to Setubal. On the Monday night some 300 of the townsmen had been to Alcacer and won back the artillery that the Spanish Captain Acosta had taken from them.

With the loss of eleven men the Portuguese wounded three or four Spanish and took two prisoners. Encouraged by this, the people of Alcacer cried for King Don Antonio and took up arms against the garrison in the castle, which was commanded by Captain Villa Gomez. By the time the Duke of Alva sent troops to rescue they found the place abandoned.

The Spanish did arrive at Setubal on 16th and laid siege, their passage to the sea was secured by Prior Don Ernando. The Duke of Alva set out the artillery on the 17th and on his demand the town surrendered immediately. Artillery and armaments were discovered, and besides the townspeople there were about 500

French and English present. However, the duke decided that there was no need to occupy the town.

On 19th he went to inspect the fort of Oton where, he was informed, there were 400 Portuguese soldiers prepared to die rather than surrender. Spanish cannon were deployed but resistance was stiff. The defenders had three galleons nearby to assist them that inflicted several fatalities. The artillery battery began on the 20th, on the arrival of Spanish reinforcements two of the galleons surrendered, but the fort and the remaining galleon continued to resist. After receiving a heavy battering it attempted to shelter under protection of fort's walls.

As the Duke de Alva carried on the campaign Philip felt so confident of success that he returned to Spain. Don Antonio in Lisbon was reported to be short of everything and likely to retreat to Santarem. Belated support was on its way from France, as twelve French captains with a supply of arms were sent to Portugal while a resume of situation was sent to Walsingham.

Contrary to the Spanish view, a rumour was spread that King Henry III of France would declare war on Spain if Philip did not withdraw his troops. Don Antonio's forces said to number 40,000 but very few were trained soldiers. Against them Philip's army consisted of 24,000 foot and some one thousand horse, although they too were supposed to be short of provisions in a poor country. The Portuguese were resisting strongly, in one of the towns they had retaken taken, 300 ordinary Spanish soldiers were reputed to have been killed, and the fate of commander was not known. The Portuguese had also taken two Spanish ships coming from Peru.

Ambassador Mendoza in London was instructed to tell Queen Elizabeth that Philip not only had the right to the Portuguese throne but the power and the joyful support of the people. Elizabeth reaffirmed that she would not involve herself in the affairs of anyone whose right had not been acknowledged, but even so, she kept probing Mendoza for another four hours during their interview over the matter, in particular Don Antonio's proclamation as King of Portugal.

Antonio de Castillo, who had represented Portugal at the English court since the time of Cardinal King Henry, was still there on the authority of the five governors, from whom he had not heard for six months. At first his stance was that, until they sent him word as to who was the rightful king he could not recognise anyone, including Don Antonio, although there was the fact that Cardinal King Henry was known to have declared him to be illegitimate with no right to the throne. But De Castillo had since heard that the governors had acknowledged Philip as king of Portugal. Confusion reigned, 1,000 Scots were rumoured to be getting ready to go to Portugal, Don Antonio's agent, Juan Rodriguez de Souza, was in London, and ships had left with munitions for Portugal but they were being detained by contrary weather.

Dr Ruy Lopez, one of Elizabeth's court physicians, wrote from Walsingham House to her favourite, Robert Dudley, Earl of Leicester, that the ambassador from Don Antonio had asked Elizabeth for twelve ships with arms, munitions, 2,000 arquebuses and officers, as much bronze ordnance as her Majesty could spare, 1,000 quintals of powder and 2,000 quintals of iron balls of every sort. The payment to be made in Portugal in coin, jewels, or whatever Elizabeth requested.

Material support for Don Antonio was forthcoming from the Portuguese clergy, who presented him with jewels and plate from churches and monasteries, and he was reported to be well accompanied by nobility. However, it was generally believed that Philip had the upper hand. The Spanish army was approaching Lisbon, which, they bragged, they were confident of taking.

The French consul left Lisbon on 10th August with a plea to King Henry of France and Catherine the Queen Mother to increase their aid, the French had sent only 400 expert captains. Opinion was that Lisbon was a lost cause, but Don Antonio assured them he had plenty of support elsewhere in the country, that Lisbon was not the whole country and the capital would take a lot of defending.

King Philip was intending to place his son Don Diego on the Portuguese throne, but was being delayed by having to fight Don Antonio. Prince Diego, heir to Philip as king of Spain and Portugal, was five years old and he died of small pox aged seven in 1582.

Fernando Alvarez de Toldeo, the much-feared Duke of Alva swept down on Lisbon, as he had done years before in the Netherlands, and reportedly crushed the life out of Portuguese patriotism for, unlike the Netherlands, there was no religious cause to fight for, and no William of Orange to command the patriots here. A critic wrote that the Portuguese were made from different stuff from the stubborn Dutchmen, and so Alva was able to ride roughshod over them with little resistance.

Fernando Álvarez de Toledo, Duke de Alva

On the 25th August Don Antonio with an army of somewhere between 9,000 and 23,000, reports, or propaganda, varied widely, gave battle at Alcantara to the west of Lisbon, but he was outmanoeuvred and defeated by the Duke de Alva's army of 50,000. An estimated combined total of 8,000 were slain. Don Antonio, after supposedly fighting more like a private soldier than a king, left the field of battle only after all was lost. He was injured either with two sword cuts to the head or with a wound to the neck, reports differ. He entered Lisbon but left immediately by another gate for fear of betrayal and went "no man knows whither" as it was thought, but actually north east to Santarem, arriving on 27th August with many supporters.

Duke de Alva took the city of Lisbon by force on the same day, the 25th, where the people submitted and sent him the keys to the city gates. On the River

Tagus, Philip's naval commander, Santa Cruz, captured seven great ships of Don Antonio's that were in the port of Lisbon. Disappointingly for Don Antonio, despite his believed popularity, no one came forward to defend Lisbon on his behalf. The one-time claimant to the throne, the Duke of Braganza, did not intervene on either side.

The merchants of Lisbon gave the Duke of Alva 60,000 ducats to save the city from being ransacked, the soldiers of the Duke having already ransacked the suburbs and the countryside for thirty miles around to the estimated value of two million and more. Spanish propaganda put it about that the people of Lisbon thought this cheap at the price for being saved from Don Antonio. The Duke of Alva departed, leaving his illegitimate son, Prior Don Ernando, as governor. Don Ernando was the Governor of Catalonia, a member of Council for State and of War, Captain General of Cavalry, and Prior of the Military Order of Malta in Castile and Leon. But in some quarters it was rumoured that Lisbon had fallen due more to corruption by promises and presents than by the activities and the skill of Alva.

On the following Sunday morning Don Antonio left Santarem with 200 horse and about 1,000 foot. He stopped and slept overnight nine miles away from the town and on the next day continued north to Tomar, where he was joined by more cavalry and 2,000 foot. From Tomar he went to Coimbra with more men joining him on the way.

King Philip was known to be in poor health, so to give encouragement to Don Antonio's cause, a rumour was circulated that Philip was dead. He was actually ill for fourteen days. On the other side there were rumours from the Spanish, false propaganda spread to demoralise his supporters, that Don Antonio had been killed.

Ambassador Mendoza sent congratulations to his king, while from England Elizabeth sent a letter to Don Antonio offering her sympathy and verbal support, but no offer of practical help. Juan Rodriguez de Souza, his agent, was working hard on his behalf; he offered a collar of precious stones to Leicester but Leicester refused it. He offered Government Secretary Wilson some jewels and tried to negotiate with him and Walsingham, but they advised him that any aid that could be sent would be too late, and that the Indies and the Azores offered more hope.

William of Orange told Elizabeth that if she gave help to Don Antonio then he would send twenty-two armed ships from Holland. Then, late in the day,

Elizabeth gave a commission to William Hawkins, the brother of John Hawkins, "to have charge of a fleet of ships to be employed on a voyage of discovery on the coasts of Africa and America." In addition she pointedly gave him authority, "to assist Don Antonio, King of Portugal, against any of his enemies." Taking this opportunity, De Souza tried to encourage the recently-returned Francis Drake personally to attack the West Indies and Brazil.

On the 18th of September, Ambassador Cobham wrote to Walsingham that Portugal should serve as a warning to all states that considered opposing King Philip. Two days later he wrote that there was no further certain news from Portugal, but that all was "overthrown and lost through the treason of the Governors." At the English court a newcomer, Cavaliero Giraldo, was not acceptable to Philip as the Portuguese ambassador because he had been appointed by Don Antonio.

The events on the Iberian Peninsular were soon left far from the thoughts of English people. Francis Drake had returned on the 26th of September after an absence of almost three years, from what had turned out to be a very profitable circumnavigation of the globe, and with the comforting knowledge that Spain, with its dominions and its valuable shipping, was vulnerable.

Too late in the day for Don Antonio, aid arrived in Portugal from France. Two ships and 300 soldiers landed at Viana, in the extreme north, but they were far too late, and so they returned to Nantes. However, the French King Henry and the Queen Mother Catherine de Medici regarded Philip's actions in Portugal as unjust and intended to continue with their aid for Don Antonio. Catherine in particular became his most loyal and consistent supporter.

It was reported that King Philip was treating the Portuguese lightly and that the Portuguese people had been completely subdued, however this was far from the truth. The Spaniards proclaimed Don Antonio a bastard and a rebel, and a great price was set upon his head. A story was put out that he was a fugitive, being hunted from town to town, holding out for weeks in one fortress, only to be starved into another. In reality, Don Antonio and his army of 12,000 men had retreated to the mountains.

From there they took by force the castle of Feira, south of Oporto, which had been reinforced by a large number of Spanish troops. They then took and sacked the coastal town of Aveiro, where the leading men were beheaded as punishment for surrendering to Philip. This made Don Antonio confident enough to move further south to a town twelve miles from Coimbra.

For whatever reason, he then changed his mind and instead went north to Oporto which he took on 16th October. He went north again to capture the castle of Viana with its useful artillery. It was reported that he held most of the country there and had a force of 30,000 men. In private Queen Elizabeth very pleased with this news and considered giving practical help in the form of ships and troops, but Don Antonio had sufficient men, it was powder and munitions that he lacked. He also had the firm support of the clergy and possession of the coastal cities of Oporto and Viana, but the general view in Spain was that, although his position in the north seemed secure for the time being, it was only a small part of the country that supported him, and his hopes of success were small unless he could hold out until help came from France.

From Oporto Don Antonio sent 20,000 crowns to France to buy more munitions, he wrote to King Henry that he was quite healed of his wounds and that the Spanish version of events was to be ignored. The Queen Mother was particularly enthusiastic in her support for him, and she was thinking to arrange a marriage for him to one of her nieces. On King Henry's instructions 300 or 400 men with munitions were sent to Rouen to be ready for Don Antonio's service. Don Antonio wrote to Filippo di Strozzi, the Marshal of France, who as a young man had been to Scotland to fight for Mary Queen of Scots, to enlist his cooperation. It was believed that his forces in Portugal could hold out until French troops arrived to support them but while on their way the French ships were driven back by a storm.

The Duke of Alva moved north and on 21st October arrived at Oporto where he swiftly defeated Don Antonio's forces. The towns of Oporto and Viana and other towns in the region then surrendered. Don Antonio himself had been accidentally hurt in the arm and face by the pike of one of his own men; he fled via Coimbra to Monte Maior, "a strong place" to the east of Viana. The Count de Benevente and Count de Lemos with 20,000 men, a figure almost certain to be an exaggeration, were sent to take it.

The blame for Don Antonio's defeat was laid at the door of one man, his ambassador at Oporto, Francesco Baretto, who was thought to have betrayed him for the price of 11,000 ducats. Baretto was caught and put to death in Coimbra.

To the outside world Don Antonio's position was unclear, it was even believed that there was small hope that he was even alive. No one knew for certain what had become of him after his flight from Oporto and Viana. The

Spanish heard news that he was in the mountains with 7,000 or 8,000 men, but that "no great credit can be given it."

All the same, Philip was cautious, he took these unsettling reports seriously, working on the assumption that Don Antonio was still very strong and that he had Frenchmen with him. He recalled the troops he had dismissed when he had thought that possession of the country was assured and made his way to Lisbon with 8,000 men.

The army of Don Antonio had dispersed after the defeat at Oporto and on 22nd October he fled north to Viana, where he was hidden for three days in a tavern, or cookshop. Here he was again betrayed but he escaped at night with his servants. They separated and although his servants were captured Don Antonio escaped by hiding in rushes. He became a fugitive similar to Bonnie Prince Charlie after Culloden in a later century, protected by locals and peasants, working his way south until he arrived at Lisbon, where friends arranged his escape by sea to France.

Conflicting stories were in circulation, by one of them Don Antonio was believed to have been captured or killed in the battle at Oporto, by another many believed that, although he had been defeated in the battle, he was not only alive and free but still in possession of the towns of Oporto and Viana, where he was reported to be very strong and doing "much harm to the Spaniards."

The stories of the defeat and death of Don Antonio were not altogether believed, his cause was reported to be still flourishing, but whatever the case, King Philip's growing strength made Don Antonio's cause more doubtful.

Philip was accepted as King of Portugal at Tomar, to the north-east of Lisbon beyond Santarem, but the people of the city of Lisbon excused themselves from allegiance to him because they had already sworn loyalty to Don Antonio. Lisbon was now in the possession of the Spaniards, where its citizens particularly hated the occupation because of the behaviour of the soldiers; houses were spoiled, wives and children were "misused," and affrays between Portuguese and Spanish soldiers were an everyday occurrence. At the same time, the raging sickness was causing many deaths, especially among Spaniards.

Philip at this time was suffering in his personal life. His fourth and last wife, Anna of Austria, died in childbirth with Princess Maria on 26th October. While grieving for his wife Philip also fell ill.

On the 3rd of December the total defeat of Don was proclaimed, and on the 5th King Philip himself, now recovered, re-entered Portugal for the coronation in

Lisbon of his five-year old second son, Don Diego, Prince of Asturias, as king of Portugal. Then, as if in an attempt to end all speculation, a rumour went around that Philip had had Don Antonio secretly put to death in prison.

King Philip, being an extremely religious monarch, saw the conquest of Portugal as divine providence, but the reality, of course, was more prosaic, he had achieved his aim by military might and political scheming. So, in 1580, Portugal and its empire were added to Spain, the Portuguese were the leading maritime nation and the best navigators of the Atlantic seaways, and the annexation not only added the Portuguese empire to that of Spain, but also its fleet of excellent ships that made Spain now a first-rate naval power. Proof of this was to come later with two successful defeats of French fleets fighting on behalf of Don Antonio at the islands of the Azores. However, in addition to the benefits, there were some disadvantages, for example there were more places around the world for Spain to defend.

As for Don Antonio, his reign as King of Portugal has lasted only a matter of weeks, yet, despite this, his supporters viewed Philip's success not as a total defeat but only a setback to the rightful cause.

1581

In England

In January 1581 Don Antonio, Prior of Crato, was nowhere to be found in Portugal, even though 20,000 ducats were offered for him dead or alive. News told that he was in France, while at the same time it was rumoured that he was still in arms near the border with Andalucia. There was word that he was seeking help from the Dutch rebels, while yet another rumour was believed in Spain that he had fled to North Africa, where he was also attempting to get help. This latter story gained some credence as people of the Algarve in the south of Portugal revolted against Philip in favour of Don Antonio, and across the Straits likewise along the north African coast, at Tangier, Ceutra and Masagao.

Queen Elizabeth sent word to the Portuguese islands of the Azores encouraging them to stand by Don Antonio, but then, on the 16th January, an Englishman arrived in France to join Don Antonio, who had arrived in Brittany from Portugal in disguise and in want of money.

Juan de Souza, who had been Don Antonio's agent in London, on receiving news of the second defeat of Don Antonio, evaded Spanish ships and returned to England on 21st December, where he stayed in London with Dr Ruy Lopez, Queen Elizabeth's Portuguese physician. Here the pair had to be constantly on their guard because the Spanish were very keen to find out about Don Antonio's affairs and wanted to get hold of one of De Souza's servants in order to question him.

News reached Elizabeth that Don Antonio was safe, that he had left his beloved Portugal for France, where he was being received by King Henry and Catherine the Queen Mother at Dolenville.

In public Elizabeth had betrayed annoyance at Don Antonio's assumption of the title of king, declining to help him and refusing to see his ambassadors, but in secret she sent messages of encouragement. It served her purposes that any disturbance in Portugal was to England's advantage. Edward Prinn, Elizabeth's ambassador in France, was also in favour of Don Antonio and intended to speak to the Portuguese émigrés arriving in Tours.

Conversely, Mary Queen of Scots, that thorn in Elizabeth's side, who was now in the thirteenth year of her exile and confinement in England, sent her hearty congratulations to Philip on his success in Portugal.

Confusion reigned in Europe. In Italy the opinion was that Don Antonio was dead. In France there was confusion over his whereabouts. Catherine the Queen Mother, who was reported to be "apassionated," with Don Antonio, heard a story, a false story, that he had sent a message to King Philip begging to recover his favour and be pardoned.

French ministers laughed at the idea that he was in their country, but they noticed that there was an increasing number of Portuguese in France. Filipo di Strozzi, the Marshal of France, was known to be going frequently to Tours to speak to Portuguese gentlemen at a time when Don Antonio was believed to be alive and well in Portugal. Di Strozzi would soon become the most ardent and talented of Don Antonio's generals.

Wherever Don Antonio was, he did not feel safe in France, he was known to wish to come to England to meet Elizabeth, but from her point of view he was not such an attractive prospect because he did not have money, although he did have jewels.

In the spring of 1581 Don Antonio was supposed to be in Mazagao on the Barbary coast but he was expected to leave there for Bordeaux. He wrote to Queen Elizabeth that he was in secure place safe from his enemies and in good health; she replied that she wished to assist him in going to France. A Portuguese noble, Count Francisco de Vimioso, was acting as agent for Don Antonio, travelled through Portugal disguised as a priest, bringing news to encourage support for him in France. De Vimioso obtained an audience with their French majesties. Together they discussed ways to aid Don Antonio's cause that were the "conditions to be propounded to the King of Portugal," among which was the treatment of vessels owing allegiance to Don Antonio, and the raising of troops in August to assist in taking the islands of the Azores, while Marshal Di Strozzi expressed his preference for a voyage to Portugal itself.

In Spain people were still learning about the circumstances of the attempted capture of Don Antonio in Lisbon. In Portugal, where the Spanish feared a rising by the people, the search was still going on for him. Among the stories in circulation there was some doubt about his being in France, because if he were there then his presence would have been discovered by King Philip's spies. On the other hand, some did believe that he was secretly in France, together with the Portuguese crown jewels and gold, believed to be worth about two million crowns, and, furthermore, that he had written to Elizabeth's French suitor, Francis of Valois, the Duke of Alencon, or Monsieur as he was popularly known, to request the support of King Henry.

Although mainland Portugal had been largely subdued, the Portuguese Indies had not yet declared for Philip, while in the Portuguese islands of the Azores the Spaniards had more reason for concern.

The archipelago of the Azores lies in the Atlantic 950 miles, or 1525km, to the west of Portugal. It consists of nine islands, San Miguel, with its capital Ponta del Garda (290 sq.m.), Pico (173 sq.m.), Terceira (153 sq.m.), San Jorge (94 sq.m.), Faial (67 sq.m.), Flores (55 sq.m.), Santa Maria (37 sq.m.), Graciosa (23 sq.m.), and tiny Corvo (7 sq.m.). Although Terceira was not the largest island it was the most important, being the port of call for ships crossing the Atlantic and en route to India. It was the administrative, economic, and religious centre of the Azores and an exchange place for gold, silver, diamond and spices. As a result of this it was militarily sensitive and it was attacked constantly by pirates and corsairs.

In England a proposal was put forward for ships to go to the Azores in support of Don Antonio, conditional on his agreement. The first proposed enterprise was for a landing on Terceira, with a second fleet to continue round the Cape of Good Hope to Calicut in India, and there to establish a trade for spices in partnership with Don Antonio, King of Portugal. An estimate of costs was prepared for an English fleet of eight ships and four pinnaces to sail in the service of Don Antonio under the command of the newly-knighted Sir Francis Drake. The fleet, with victuals for four months, was to set out on 15th June to the Azores and to go on to Portugal if called upon.

While Elizabeth was now demonstratively supportive of Don Antonio she was very much aware that she was in danger of incurring the anger of King Philip.

In mainland Portugal the plague had run its course, but there was now famine, and Lisbon was in need of wheat – from England. Bernardino de Mendoza, the Spanish ambassador to London, was advised not to deal with Elizabeth but only directly with merchants.

Philip's policy in Portugal was one of appeasement; on 15th April he declared an amnesty for all those who had participated in what he called Don Antonio's "rebellion," although there were to be exceptions. When Don Antonio had been forced to leave Portugal Frenchmen in Lisbon had been arrested by the Spanish and tortured to reveal how he had been helped to escape.

Propaganda at the time was circulated that Philip was trying hard to agree with Don Antonio, offering him Calabria and Puglia from the Spanish possessions at the foot of Italy, or else the Indies, and threatening that if he disagreed then all Spain, Portugal and France would be against him. But even if this story were true, was it sincere or was it simply a delaying tactic? Because, at Hiers-Brouage near La Rochelle on the Atlantic coast of France, preparations were being made for transport of munitions to aid Don Antonio's cause, and Di Strozzi held a commission to raise 8,000 men and six ships to sail from La Rochelle. If Don Antonio was in France then Philip wanted him to leave.

Elizabeth received a request from the people of the island of Terceira for assistance in holding the island for Don Antonio. The islanders offered to pay for any arms sent, after which they could receive Don Antonio from North Africa, where they believed him to be. They offered the additional inducement that the Azores could provide an English base for Drake and others like him. Elizabeth was continually considering ways of how to resist Philip's growing strength; one way was to assist Don Antonio, another was to consider English involvement in the Spanish Netherlands, otherwise called the Low Countries. But she hesitated in giving aid to Don Antonio until more was known from France. The French were doing what they could, and Count Vimioso wished to travel to England to meet Elizabeth to inform her personally of the state of affairs. The French-sponsored expedition was ready; Di Strozzi had gone to prepare the ships and Don Antonio was thought to be at La Rochelle, having arrived by ship the previous week.

In England hatred towards Spain was growing, so with this mood to influence her, Queen Elizabeth agreed to help with English ships to the value of £40,000 when it seemed that Don Antonio was unlikely to get anything more from France. She suggested forming a league with France to help him, but she would not assist or meddle in his affairs until she knew what the French were doing.

Rumours that reached the French court were that Don Antonio was in France, perhaps in Brittany, perhaps in Normandy, but then he could be in England. Catherine the Queen Mother was strongly in favour of his claim, although she regretted his leaving for England if that report were true. However, some reports said that he was still in France. The deception continued as to his whereabouts. He was thought not to be in England after all, and that a person there who had taken his name was a decoy.

It was to Don Antonio's advantage that there should be doubt of his whereabouts. Then news came that he was in England after all. He had sailed from Calais on the 22nd June and on his arrival, even though Elizabeth feared it would invite revenge by Philip, he was nevertheless welcomed by the queen and the Earl of Leicester.

Dr Ruy Lopez had known for a fact that Don Antonio was in England, that he had landed at Dover with ten Portuguese disguised as sailors and posing as his own messenger as far as Rochester. Ambassador Mendoza discovered through his informants that Don Antonio was in a town not far from London with an entourage that now reportedly numbered fourteen persons. It was said that he had already been twice to London to speak to the queen but this was not certain. Mendoza issued a description of Don Antonio that he was "under the middle height, with a thin face and very dark, the hair and beard being somewhat grey, and the eyes green."

When Don Antonio arrived in the "town not far from London," which was in fact Stepney, two miles from Greenwich, he regarded himself as not fit to be seen by the queen after all his travails. Mendoza recorded that "for lack of apparel he will not demand audience (with Elizabeth) these two days." But on 1st July Walsingham wrote to Burghley that "the strange guest" had had a royal audience the previous night, and that this guest had requested ten ships to take him to the isle of Terceira.

Confirmation of Don Antonio being in England, but supposedly with only two companions, a chamberlain and a servant, was received by Philip who made a complaint to Elizabeth about her acceptance of the "rebel" and the aid given to him and the Comte de Vimioso. He ended his complaint by hoping that Elizabeth would reject Don Antonio and his claims. Mendoza asked Elizabeth to arrest Don Antonio as a rebel but she demurred, saying that although she was undecided whether or not to help him, she would certainly not arrest him or kill him. In actual fact it had been she who had lodged him at the house in Stepney and at her meeting with him, Leicester, Drake, Walsingham, Winter and Hawkins were present.

While in conversation with the Earl of Leicester, Don Antonio revealed that he had been hiding in the town of Tomar, some sixty or seventy miles north of Lisbon, a town where Juan, Duke of Braganza, previously one of the rival claimants for the throne, was constable on Philip's behalf, and when the Cortes of Tomar had confirmed Philip's coronation, he had been present in the crowd that had taken the oath of allegiance. He added that he had had to pay 20,000 crowns in total to the people who had helped him in his escape.

Don Antonio asked Queen Elizabeth to take him under her protection. He emphasised his legitimacy and protested his right to the Portuguese throne even if he had been a bastard, citing precedents of other bastards who had inherited the crown. He might have named Elizabeth and her half sister Mary, who had both been made illegitimate by their own father. Illegitimacy was simply a technicality that could be overcome. Don Antonio was to repeat his claim to Elizabeth on more than one occasion.

Queen Elizabeth I of England

He requested twelve ships, to be "well found with artillery, men and munition," 2,000 arquebusiers, bronze artillery, 1,000 quintals gunpowder, 2,000 iron balls of every sort. He had personally bought £700 worth of munitions. The repayment, he promised, was to be made in Portugal when he had been installed as king. As king of Portugal, Don Antonio was able to boast that he commanded all the gold in the fort of St. George of Amina, a Portuguese territory on the coast of Ethiopia, and it could be delivered to Queen Elizabeth's agents and representatives to be brought for her use.

With the promise of hard cash, Elizabeth commissioned ships for the task, while Portuguese ships were ordered by Don Antonio to put themselves at the disposal of the two monarchs, and if the fleet were to meet any ships of King Philip they had Queen Elizabeth's and King Antonio's permission to take them.

With regard to the fleet requested by the Terceiran islanders, Elizabeth consented to supply warships and 4,000 men, armed and victualled for three months, to sail to the Azores. Don Antonio offered to repay her within one month and made other concessions. On the wider world stage, he informed her, treaties had been made with the Sultan of Turkey, the Shereef of Morocco, and the King of France. Elizabeth consulted Drake about the fleet but it was not possible to have the ships ready by the anticipated time, the 6th June, and it was also contrary to the winds of the season on which all sails depended.

Nevertheless, two or three ships had already sailed to the Azores with arms, and four more were ready, the largest of which was 300 tons and the smallest 100 tons, the fitting out of which was being carried on in a great hurry and 500 men in area of Plymouth had been recruited by a secret order from Elizabeth and the council.

In London, Mendoza was fully aware of the preparations, so, in an attempt to deter the expedition, he spread rumours that King Philip had ordered forty galleons to be sent to go to punish Terceira. This frightened and deterred the remainder of the English ships, and Mendoza followed up this successful propaganda by adding more about how difficult it would be to hold the island and that there was a lack of shelter for ships.

King Philip had actually sent his ship, the *Gallion,* of 400 tons, with written pardons for citizens of the Azores, where all the islands had acquiesced except Terceira. It was in Terceira where the people had refused admission to Philip's governor. Aid from England was to be sent to the island immediately, it consisted of the four ships under Drake that were ready and waiting at Plymouth. This prompted Mendoza to repeat his false warning about the fictitious Spanish galleons and troops.

Don Antonio was too valuable a card in Elizabeth's hand to be let go. She made the most of him, treating him with royal honours and calling him by the title of King of Portugal. Part of the attraction, although he had no actual money, were the Portuguese crown jewels, the spoils of the East and West Indies, that Don Antonio had brought with him in the care of Count Vimioso. Don Antonio also assured Elizabeth that he had one million in money and more jewels hidden in Portugal.

Elizabeth and her courtiers were susceptible to greed and so, with the promise of gold and jewels as security, money for loans for the warlike preparations, the purchase of ships, and the payments for troops and victuals, was rapidly forthcoming. Don Antonio seems to have been trusting and generous to the point of naivety in making presents of the crown jewels, giving some of the best to Elizabeth and Leicester and pledging many to the London merchants, most of which ultimately arrived somehow in the queen's hands.

In Spain and Portugal, meanwhile, stories true and false about Don Antonio abounded, among which were; that a loan of 200,000 crowns was on its way from an Italian merchant in Terceira; that Don Antonio was issuing letters of marque (a licence for armed ships to take enemy merchantmen), against Philip; that he was to take a fleet from England against Philip; that those the ships might go on to Brazil; that English and Portuguese were being sent as spies on Don Antonio's behalf; that Mendoza knew of a secret mail system between England and Lisbon; that Elizabeth had given £5,000 and munitions for Don Antonio's fleet; that in England it was now openly said that Don Antonio was the rightful king of Portugal; that, although Don Antonio had gone from Calais to England to talk to Elizabeth, it was believed he would return to France.

On receiving help from France and the encouraging news of Don Antonio, the Azores rose in revolt. In retaliation the Spanish soldiers seized some Portuguese officers and cut others to pieces.

The Spanish commander, Pietro de Valdez, with six hundred men sent by Philip, landed in the islands "to keep the Azores in allegiance," and built a fort. On the 25th July, the feast day of Santiago, St. James the warrior saint, the patron saint of Spain, the battle of the Bay of Salga in Terceira took place. In this a militia of Terceiranses and French with some Portuguese, totalling 6,000 defenders with some cannon, repelled the Spanish force. And much more than being repelled, De Valdez was rumoured to have been cut to pieces along with all his men.

When this news reached England it spurred Don Antonio to hasten the dispatch of his ships, he was pinning his hopes on keeping the Azores, from where he could seize and plunder Spanish ships, in particular the Spanish India fleet.

Elizabeth now allowed Don Antonio to have free rein. He appointed a governor general for the Azores, Juan Francisco of Portugal, who was due to depart from France within the next few days.

The supply and fitting out of Don Antonio's fleet continued. It was intended that twenty-five ships were to go with Drake, now known as the famous corsair, as the admiral. The ships' captains went to meet Don Antonio to receive orders, but it appeared that it was to be more of a voyage of plunder in his name, with only twenty persons of note from Portugal on board.

In Portugal some couriers of Don Antonio were found and arrested, and while Philip was making ready twenty ships and 3,500 men in Seville to go to the Azores, he again wrote personally to Elizabeth claiming that Don Antonio was a rebel subject. "I beg, therefore," he asked, "as I have done before, that you will take steps at once to have Don Antonio handed over to me," in other words, to his ambassador Mendoza.

Despite the enthusiasm for the Azores enterprise, the arming of Don Antonio's ships was going very slowly. His fleet so far totalled only eight, and even then, though Don Antonio saw Elizabeth nearly every day, she changed her ever-fickle mind to allow only two of his ships and a pirate ship to depart with stores for only two months and only sufficient men to plunder at sea.

Elizabeth said she would not on any account make war with King Philip, this prompted Don Antonio to ask for the return of the jewels he had pledged to Walsingham, who refused to do so except on the payment of £3,000. Some of the Portuguese crown jewels had been left with Walsingham for safety, and when Don Antonio made his demand Walsingham alleged that he had been personally responsible for purchasing some of the provisions that Don Antonio had ordered, and made difficulties about giving them up.

In disgust Don Antonio lost faith in Elizabeth and tried to sell his ships, at which the queen relented, she changed her mind again to let seven ships sail, including four pirates, whose captains were to be Portuguese, to take 100 soldiers in the largest ship and 60 to 80 in the others, to land on Terceira if the people were in favour. So Don Antonio once more made ready to sail and then Elizabeth prevaricated yet again and delayed his departure. A golden opportunity was slipping away.

Finally, fourteen ships under the command of Drake were sent by King Henry of France to secure the Azores for Don Antonio. Other corsairs joined in but the fleet was defeated by the Spaniards.

In his correspondence with King Philip, Mendoza, writing from London, explained the jewels for loans situation; "The queen lent Don Antonio £3,000 when he was here, and I understand she peremptorily demands payment of the sum, taking possession of the diamond which was pledged here for a sum of £5,000 lent by the merchants, who offer to relinquish their claim to the queen, if she will lend them £3,000 free of interest for six years out of the bars brought by Drake, which they will repay in five yearly instalments of £6,000 each. So far as I can learn, this talk of a loan is a mere fiction and a cloak under which the queen may keep the diamond for the £8,000 on the ground that the merchants advanced the £5,000 by her express order, without which they would not have done so. This plan was invented by Cecil in order to prevent Don Antonio from getting his diamond back again."

The diamond in question was described as being of the purest sort, with a large pearl pendant. It weighed eight carats and was called the Portuguese from its having been one of the crown jewels of Portugal.

It was at this time that intrigues over Don Antonio began in earnest Elizabeth's court. Dr Ruy Lopez, as Don Antonio's go-between and interpreter at court, was accused of making a good thing out of the negotiations until money began to run short, at which point, so his accusers had it, he went over to King Philip to sell his knowledge there, and he was believed to have attempted to poison Don Antonio on more than one occasion. Don Antonio was surrounded by spies though it was said "he knew it not." But he definitely found that he was being frustrated, betrayed, and defrauded in every way in England, while all the time his store of precious jewels was dwindling.

Undeterred, in September he bought two ships with the intention of equipping twenty more, but his financiers wanted security. He had the jewels valued but they were deemed to be worth not more than 36,000 crowns, which was insufficient and therefore the vessels could not sail. He had already applied to Elizabeth for help but she had as yet made no decision.

Two weeks later Don Antonio was still being deferred while being pressed to part with more jewels in order to pay the debts he had already incurred, and then, as security, to borrow a further £12,000. Elizabeth did speak to the richest men in London to encourage them to lend, stressing Don Antonio's right to the throne, but everyone, including Elizabeth herself, still looked for excuses to delay him. In short, so long as the money lasted he could spend it in England, and leave his diamonds, but whenever the suggestion arose of assembling a fleet under his banner, some specious excuse was always invented to prevent any expedition openly hostile against King Philip leaving an English port.

Finally, feeling aggrieved and betrayed, without Elizabeth's consent, Don Antonio left London on 18th September for France, even though there was a rumour was that if he went there he would be killed. "There is treason prepared in France for him, but he is obstinately bewitched to his evident ruin." He had been fleeced by the English but they wanted to keep him as a potential tool against Spain. Elizabeth outwardly attempted to stop his departure by ordering that no vessel should be allowed to leave Dover or its nearby ports, while at the same time she helped him by lending him a coach to travel there.

And all the while Ambassador Mendoza was spreading stories to discredit him. Don Antonio stayed at the house of a customs officer six miles from Dover until he could sail, his ships were waiting off the Isle of Wight but they were being detained by contrary winds. Then at last, on the 29th September, he sailed for France.

Don Antonio landed at Dieppe with five ships that he had bought in England. There he had a conference with Monsieur, Elizabeth's suitor. His staunchest allies, Count Vimioso and Di Strozzi went to meet him, but few held out any real hopes, and the Venetian ambassador to France, when writing to his master the Doge, doubted if help for Don Antonio would be forthcoming in France.

However, Don Antonio still had the remaining crown jewels and while they lasted he was treated with consideration and regal splendour in "that gay and dissolute Court." But he still seemed to be over-generous with these assets, many of which were given in bribes amongst the "easy-going ladies and painted mignons." In the end he did get a better return for them in France than he got in England. Meanwhile back in England, Queen Elizabeth, ever the parsimonious, retrieved many of the provisions that had been intended for Don Antonio's fleet.

In Spain King Philip had not eased up on his vigilance. A supporter of Don Antonio, Duarte de Castro, who had been in prison in Valladolid, was released and allowed to go to join him on condition that he would be a spy, and in Portugal King Philip inspected the fort of San Juan at the harbour in Lisbon which was then under construction.

When Don Pietro de Valdes returned to Spain from his defeat at the Bay of Salga at Terceira in the Azores he was arrested as soon as he landed. The truth of his defeat was that he had had little more than 1,000 men with which to effect a landing, and he had found the island so strongly garrisoned by French and English that he had "thought it well" not to try his luck. Then, all the while, and much to Philip's annoyance, Spanish ships were being plundered and Drake was expected to join the rebels in the Azores at any moment.

Don Antonio's seven ships left the Isle of Wight and Portsmouth on 6th October, under the command of Henry Knollys, to rendezvous at the Scilly Isles to be ready for departure to Terceira. They now had victuals for only one month, and they were short of sailors, who were beginning to desert.

Only three weeks later, on the 29th October, the ships returned from Terceira to the Isle of Wight, almost without victuals and only about 400 men in all on board, having taken arms and munitions to supply the island and bringing back funds for Don Antonio. The ships brought encouraging news, Don Antonio was assured of the island's devotion to him. 8,000 fighting men were reported to be on the island with 300 Englishmen, who were being paid, although by another account there were 100 English and 120 French soldiers. The Terceirans had written on 16th October that the island was strong enough to hold out against Spain until April, they also reported that if Don Antonio would come to the Azores the island of San Miguel, where there were no Spanish troops, would revolt.

In their anger the islanders had treated their Spanish captives barbarously and executed King Philip and the Duke of Alva in effigy. It was believed that although King Philip was now secure in Portugal he had not the means to attack the Azores. Don Antonio intended to build a fort on Terceira to strengthen his position, and in the meantime two more ships with munitions were waiting at the Isle of Wight to sail back to the island.

One way for Don Antonio to raise money was to issue letters of marque under his title of the King of Portugal, authorising his ships to capture any merchant ships with cargoes for Spain and Portugal. With this authority his ships soon took a hulk with a cargo of sugar to sell and this gave encouragement for other English ships to do the same. But the letters of marque were a source of contention because the privilege was being abused. It came to light that certain ships were raiding friendly Dutch merchantmen on the pretext of serving Don Antonio, and that pirates were also being encouraged in their activities when they learned that in Terceira the money drafts of Don Antonio were paid promptly.

In France Don Antonio was well-received, he went to Poissy to meet King Henry and Queen Mother Catherine but received no immediate assurance from them of a financial settlement. Their majesties wanted Don Antonio to marry, with the Princess of Cond being named as a prospective bride. At the end of October he received a royal visit from the king and queen before going to stay for four days at the Queen Mother's palace, where he was treated with royal honours and Catherine visited him daily.

Despite the doubters, the request to raise more troops and munitions had been duly considered and it was readily granted. In addition he was granted a pension. Many members of the French gentry entered his service as colonels, 8,000 French infantry were raised, and, it was said, 2,000 'Germans' from Flanders. Di Strozzi was appointed to be Lieutenant General and was himself making a levy of 1,000 men.

By November Don Antonio was ready to depart from Paris in order to gather his forces, although he was concerned about the cost of 30,000 crowns spent in preparation of the navy. Encouragingly, Catherine demonstrated her support and confidence by promising to pay for 3,000 soldiers and gave 15,000 crowns to the enterprise.

Ambassador Mendoza was monitoring the situation from England and he reported to Philip, not entirely accurately, that Don Antonio was trying to raise money in France by pawning more jewels, and had bought ships. He was worried that if Don Antonio did not go to the Azores and instead appeared off the coast of Portugal, he would certainly cause a popular uprising. As if to reassure himself and his sovereign, Mendoza reminded the king that when Don Antonio had gone to take Lisbon, no one would lend him money and his followers were people of no importance, and that he had gone to France "not too well satisfied" with Elizabeth and England, and that Philip's successful plots had prevented men from joining Don Antonio's cause. Mendoza further informed Philip, one imagines gleefully, that the English merchants who held some of Don Antonio's jewels had refused to send them to him in France.

Finally Philip was comforted by a general belief that Don Antonio was not very resolute in his actions and was badly served by those round him.

Meanwhile Don Antonio, who was at Tours, had sent ten companies of men to the Azores, which was sufficient for that campaign, but the Venetian ambassador to Spain commented that he would be unlikely to raise sufficient troops to attack mainland Portugal, because he had to "deal with a prince much greater than himself," and that much greater prince, King Philip, was now getting ready to "reduce" the Azores.

1582
The Azores – Part 1

Late in 1582 Don Antonio was apparently short of funds once more, the sailors on board his ships were disaffected and men were deserting, so the cargoes of sugar from Terceira, by Don Antonio's order, were taken in lieu of payment.

Ambassador Mendoza was attempting to prevent the delivery of goods valued at over 20,000 crowns from the prize ship to Don Antonio's factor, he also wished to prevent the granting of facilities for raising ships for Don Antonio, or disposing of booty acquired on his behalf. He claimed that Elizabeth had received goods from Terceira, namely sugar valued at 20,000 crowns, which was an offence against Spain. He complained that Henry Knollys, as commander of Don Antonio's ships, had been with Don Antonio's pirate ships which were taking the cargoes of sugar from ships bound for Portugal, and furthermore, that she also allowed her subjects to have letters of marque from Don Antonio but not from King Philip.

A discussion ensued about what could be regarded as morally lawful war, such as the aggressive competition between Don Antonio and King Philip, in which case the goods taken could be regarded as prizes. In the end, Elizabeth conceded that these captures were not in fact lawful and ordered Don Antonio's ships to return to port. By her order crewmen were commanded to leave those ships allowing only the captains to remain on board and an embargo was placed on the goods from Terceira by Leicester and Walsingham. So for all his trouble and effort, and his successes, Don Antonio was unlikely to gain any benefit. If ever a man was dogged by bad luck, it was Don Antonio, Prior of Crato, king of Portugal.

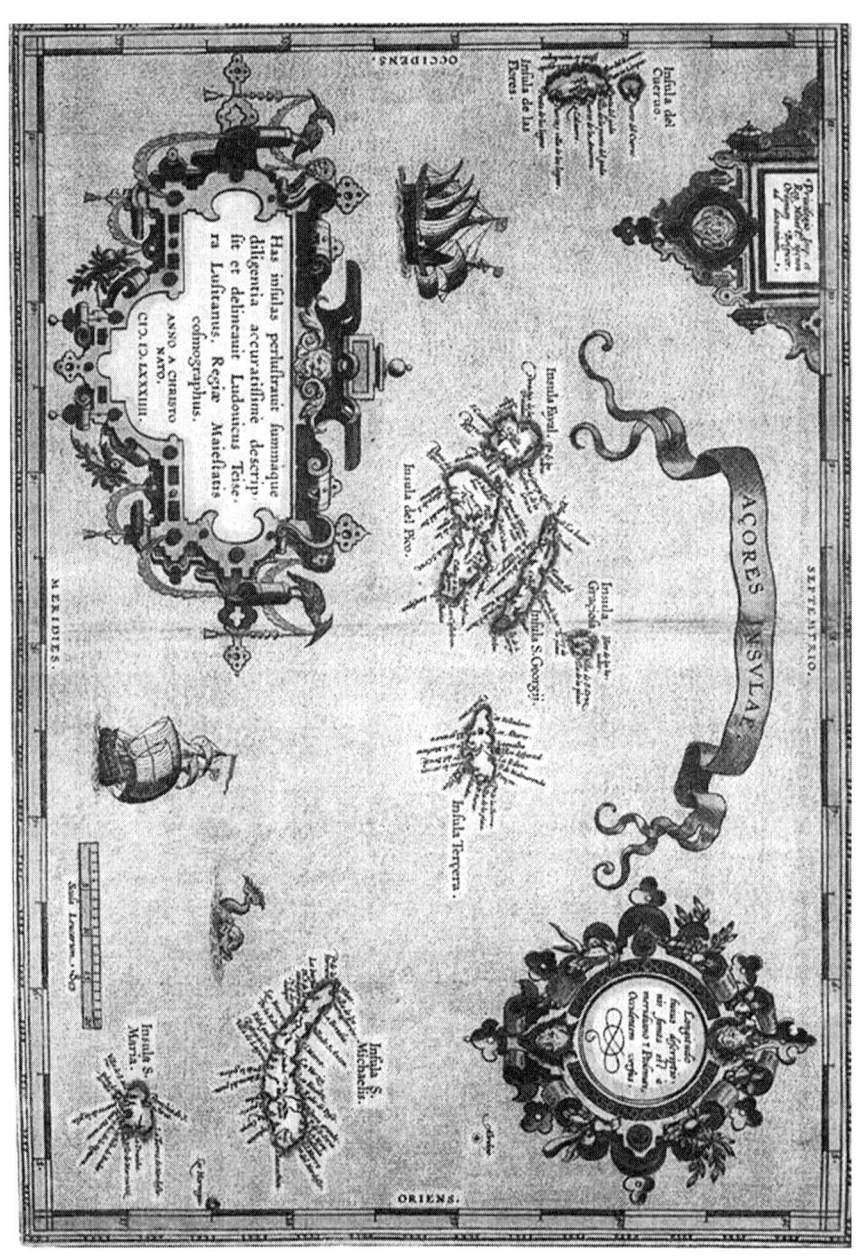

The Portuguese islands of the Azores

But not to be defeated, Don Antonio sent for help to Low Countries where The States, as the Protestant Netherlands were called, granted twelve great ships, to be manned and furnished. A proclamation was posted in Antwerp on Don Antonio's behalf, announcing that ships would not be allowed to trade with Portugal unless they held passports from his factors. However there was suspicion in Holland that Don Antonio's letters of marque issued in Terceira were being abused by pirates. To avoid an obviously intimate connection with England, two of his ships were docked away from the mainland at Isle of Wight.

There were reports of English ships plundering Dutch merchantmen on the pretext of serving Don Antonio. On the other hand his agents in Tours had detained two English captains because they had disobeyed instructions by taking Dutch ships. He asked Elizabeth what she wanted done with them.

Don Antonio's bad luck struck again when four of his ships were caught in a storm in which one of them sank. Then only days later, on 2nd February, as a result of Elizabeth's dictate, four more of his ships were detained at Plymouth and another two at Falmouth. But suddenly, as fickle as the weather itself, Elizabeth then raised the embargo and ordered all Englishmen to return to the ships or be hanged. Her intention was that they should to go to France to join Don Antonio. All was action again as sailors rejoined their ships at Plymouth, one of which in particular, the *Julian,* was to sail to Terceira with cannon and munitions.

What caused the queen's change of mind is not clear. At Plymouth the stay of Don Antonio's ships had been by royal command but the townspeople were not happy. They were financially perplexed and seeking payment for supplying the ships with victuals and stores. As ever, there was confusion when three of Don Antonio's four ships were to be allowed to sail for France, but the fourth and largest, *The White Bear,* was to remain. The three ships concerned were described as being of 100, 120 and 140 tons, one of which was labelled a pirate vessel that carried not more than 150 "persons of all sorts, a very poor array," with victuals for not more than one week.

Mendoza held meetings with Elizabeth to discuss Don Antonio, his ships and his letters of marque. He attempted to damp her encouragement for Don Antonio by saying that there was small hope that the ships which had left for France would come to anything due to the lack of money. Nevertheless the ships departed on 18th March in the charge of Diego Botelho, his agent for the Low Countries. As was often the case in the days of sailing ships, due to bad weather the little fleet had to return temporarily to Plymouth, and the departure of the *Julian* for Terceira was postponed. After another change of mind by Elizabeth, *The White Bear* was allowed to join the three and soon afterwards it captured a ship, but the cargo of sugar it took had to be returned. Don Antonio openly complained to some Germans with whom he was in contact about the treatment he had received from Elizabeth and the English.

Across the Channel in France the last detachment of troops had not yet left for the Azores, and Don Antonio held meetings in secret with the Queen Mother from which he hoped to persuade her to raise a large enough force for the invasion of Portugal. Firm and positive support was given immediately when King Henry gave Don Antonio permission to raise 6,000 foot and 500 horse in France and granted him four French ports where any goods captured under his marque could be sold, and, significantly, authority was given to mint coins at Tours for circulation in Terceira.

These events in western Europe were fully known about as far away as the eastern end of the Mediterranean. In March Murad Rey III, the Sultan of Turkey, believed that the Azores were sure to hold for Don Antonio. His grand vizier wrote to Don Antonio assuring him of the Sultan's support, and the pasha of the navy was said to have promised to take his fleet to sea. This word that the Turks were about to sail reached Lisbon, but since at that moment Turkey was at war with Persia, the sultan was unwilling to fight on two fronts, so it was unlikely to break a current truce with Philip.

England was involved indirectly in this war. Much to Mendoza's annoyance, the English were supplying tin to Turkey for the manufacture of bronze cannons and lead for ammunition. This had been going on for the previous two years by the Levant Company, the Turkey Company had been set up in 1581, that was soon to be joined by the Venice Company, established in 1583 to trade with countries of the eastern Mediterranean, notably exporting cloth to the Ottoman Empire, and tin for making cannon.

In Portugal, English and Breton ships had been harassing the coast as if in preparation for a large scale attack. Commissions from Don Antonio had been printed in Portugal for people who were to prepare the country to receive him and support him on his arrival. He had received many mariners into his service and was thought to have had an interview with King Henry of Navarre, which was then an independent kingdom. In England it was thought that the proclamation by King Antonio might endanger the safety of English subjects in

Portugal, so Walsingham was advised that safe conducts should be given to Her Majesty's subjects who traded with Spain.

This activity and the possibility that Don Antonio's forces in France might be diverted from the Azores to Portugal, caused concern in Spain, therefore Philip sent Prior Don Ernando, the son of the Duke of Alva, to Oporto to prevent a landing.

Precautionary activity in general in Portugal was stepped up, for example all foreign ships now had to be searched before leaving Lisbon, and an Englishman and a Frenchman had been captured who were believed to be spying on Don Antonio's behalf. Yet, despite these measures, an English merchant ship had managed to take some Portuguese merchants and their families from Lisbon to join Don Antonio.

Repressive measures were also taken by the Spaniards; when students in the town of Coimbra to the north of Lisbon rose in favour of King Antonio, King Philip had them cruelly executed. Then there was Don Antonio's large family, many of whom had remained in Portugal. Seven of his daughters were taken from there to Spain to be imprisoned in a nunnery where they lived "in desperation."

Don Antonio's cooks, who had been arrested by the Spanish, were released at the instigation of Philip's ministers on condition that they went from Portugal rejoin his entourage and poison him. However they were caught by Don Antonio's agents and, like any who plotted against him, they were "broken on the wheel."

On Terceira his position strengthened day by the day, his representative, Manuel de Silva, was received there with a canopy and a procession, acting as if he were the king, and metal was sent for minting into coins.

There was increasing activity along the Atlantic seaboard of France. Three ships arrived at Nantes from Terceira with goods to the value of 100,000 crowns and more, but for some reason they were not expected to be for Don Antonio. The four ships under the command of Diego de Botelho had arrived at Belle Isle off the south coast of Brittany. Further south at Bordeaux, ships for Don Antonio were ready and an army was expected under the command of De Lansac, who was also due to arrive. Early in May, ships commanded by Filipo di Strozzi arrived boldly on Spain's northern coast and landed 2,000 men in Don Antonio's name, "who burn and spoil all." It was reported that the town of Laredo, to the east of Santander had been taken.

For all this, Don Antonio succumbed to a bout of depression. From Tours he wrote a humble, almost servile, letter, not as assertive as a king ought to be, to Walsingham, who reassured him of his good affection towards him. He complained that his affairs in France were not going so well as expected, as his agent, Antonio de Vega, would inform him. His affairs were proceeding slowly due to lack of money, even in Terceira he believed his credit was small.

It was commented on that his companions spent any money he accumulated, and that he was credulous and generous towards them. Progress was certainly very slow for the eight or ten ships being fitted out at La Rochelle because there was no money. Nor were there men sufficient to defend Terceira and the other islands, nor to attack the Spanish Indies fleets.

But at last all was ready, the ships from Bordeaux sailed down the River Garonne to Hiers-Brouage near La Rochelle, where, as the Spanish knew, there were forty-two more ships with 4,000 or 5,000 men. Although the Spaniards had little certain news of Don Antonio's progress, they knew he was reported to be short of money and other things. The troops of Count Charles II de Cosse, Count Brissac, left with ships and men for Belle Isle, where the fleet was gathering. Two weeks later eight ships with 1,000 men and another two with victuals left La Rochelle, with two or three more due to follow with 800 men.

Don Antonio had requested from Elizabeth 2,000 English soldiers with their pay and victuals for one month, backing up his letters with promises of profits to come. Through Edward Prinn, Elizabeth gave permission in secret for English ships to join the fleet.

Don Antonio presented a book to Elizabeth that he wished to dedicate to her about the various titles of the competitors to the kingdom of Portugal, including his own right to the title and his descent from King Manuel the Fortunate, who had died in 1521. But always lurking in the background at the English court was Ambassador Mendoza, who informed King Philip that he had letters of Don Antonio that he intended to show Elizabeth at an advantageous moment.

King Henry's was fleet gathering at Brest, in which Don Antonio was supposed to go as its general, although this was not certain. An army was also gathering, ships from Bristol had landed English soldiers and French, numbering about 1,500, had also landed. Towards the end of May or beginning of June Di Strozzi's ships arrived at Belle Isle to join those of Count Brissac. It was reputed that now 170 ships and 7,000 men were ready, Don Antonio was to send them off personally and he might go with them. Rumours were put about to confuse the issue for the Spanish, one that the army was actually destined for Scotland to aid Mary Queen of Scots, and another that the fleet was to go to attack the fleet of Spanish Indiamen, because it was known that Don Antonio had threatened to meet the Spanish fleet on its return from the Indies.

In Terceira all was ready, an English ship had arrived with more munitions, the Count Torres de Vedra confidently told Don Antonio that he could spare 2,000 shot, all the men of Terceira, and still be able to defend the island. The viceroy of Portuguese Indies was known to be favourable to the cause and Count Vimioso was able to inform the French Queen Mother that Madeira had revolted in favour of Don Antonio.

In the conditions of the day accidents to ships were almost inevitable. News from Antwerp was that a short distance off the English coast one of the greatest ships of the fleet was completely burnt with all the munitions it carried, and of the 150 English and Portuguese on board all but four men were drowned. Burning wood was scattered by the explosion among the other ships, including the flagship which caught fire. Don Antonio, who was on board at the time, was injured in the face, at which the Spanish reported, perhaps gleefully, "They say he is dead." The explosion was believed to have been caused by "a Portuguese boy thought to frighten some soldiers, who were fetching some powder, by igniting a little, but the whole exploded."

At last the fleet was assembled, Don Antonio and Count of Vimioso, with the Portuguese nobility and three friars, joined the ships on the 15th May for a final inspection. The Spanish, always anxious to belittle Don Antonio and his cause, reported that he had left Tours at night and gone to sea with no fear of being robbed, "for he has not a penny more than a poor grey friar," and that he left all his captains behind because they were in prison for debt. Before the departure Don Antonio himself was to return first to Tours, where he had left many of his jewels in pledge, then go on to a castle of the Queen Mother near Nantes.

The fleet, with French, Dutch, English and Portuguese volunteers, sailed at about 4 a.m. on the 16th May, bound possibly for the islands in Azores that did not acknowledge Philip as their king, or possibly to mainland Portugal. As to the exact number of ships in the fleet, accounts vary between fifty and sixty, but in the event the fleet appears to have consisted of about fifty sail in all, thirty ships and twenty pattaches, which were light, fast, shallow, two-masted ships originally intended for surveillance in coastal waters. The 5,000 men on board, excluding sailors, were judged to be "good troops," fighting men, and the armaments were better than anticipated.

In the fleet were seven English ships carrying French soldiers. The army included 1,200 gentlemen, each with his own company some of which numbered thirty or forty men. Di Strozzi was the general, with Count Brissac as his lieutenant to command in his absence. Don Antonio sailed with Di Strozzi. For the first three days of the voyage, the winds and the weather were in the fleet's favour, but then it changed to rain and strong winds, making a landing in Portugal impossible.

Nevertheless, the Spanish received a report that the fleet had landed in Baiona, a small coastal town just south of Vigo in Galicia and just north of the border with Portugal, and had taken "a place of importance" with 500 soldiers, 300 gentlemen and 2,000 sailors. A few days later they had news that on the 10th July King Antonio and Di Strozzi had landed in Portugal itself and taken the town of Viana with its castle as well as two of Philip's ships.

News then came from Oporto, not far south from Viana, that a spy for Don Antonio had been seized on board a ship bound for France, but as yet there had been no confirmation of these reports and the supposition was that the country was quiet. Meanwhile in France seven more ships with 1,000 soldiers were reported to be ready to leave to supplement the force.

Superficially at least, King Philip was still supposed to be trying to come to some arrangement with Don Antonio; he had sent Rodrigo de Souza and Francisco de Costa as his ambassadors but Don Antonio had had them arrested. In France King Henry eagerly awaited news of progress, and meanwhile at the Hague, Don Antonio's agent, Diego Botelho, had commissions for ships but no money with which to fund them.

On 10th July a Spanish fleet of ninety-eight ships, carrying 15,765 men, under Admiral Alvaro de Bazan, First Marquis of Santa Cruz, known simply as Santa Cruz, left Lisbon with the general intention of meeting Don Antonio's force at Terceira, where they believed he would be on Midsummer's Eve. The army included 5,442 gentlemen and their servants, and 1,904 mariners. As a precaution a reserve had been left at Lisbon. The Spanish believed that the French and English presence in the Azores was not so numerous as they had first supposed; that the islanders were reported to be in disagreement and that a show of strength by Philip would induce them to surrender.

Philip's armada was well found in all but sailors. The Portuguese, who knew the waters and who were expected to act as pilots, had gone into hiding rather than serve against Don Antonio. The Portuguese sailors on board were there under sufferance and frequently deserted, some disguising themselves as women in order to get off the ships, while the Portuguese who remained had almost to be kept in chains to keep them on board.

So the Spanish fleet set off to search for the fleet of Don Antonio. It sailed north along the Portuguese and Spanish coasts and sighted his fleet off Finisterre in north-west Spain. The destination of the fleet was still unknown to them but it was expected with some confidence to be the Azores. The Spaniards believed that in Terceira there were 8,000 Portuguese, 1,200 French and not many fewer English, who held thirty forts. Don Antonio and his fleet, they were sure, would go there with the intention of seizing San Miguel, and then sail on to Madeira.

Don Antonio's fleet arrived in the Azores, where Di Strozzi landed with 3,000 men of French infantry on the island of San Miguel and captured it unopposed, except for 1,000 Spaniards, the garrison of a small fortress which was old and had had to be put into good repair, it was held for Philip with one month's supplies and ammunition.

On 24th July, in the midst of the rejoicings that celebrated the taking of the island, even while Di Strozzi was preparing to besiege the fort, news came from the French ships that the Spanish fleet under Santa Cruz had been sighted. The troops re-embarked in order to meet them, but the French on board seemed reluctant to attack.

The first battle between the fleets took place on 24th, in which Don Antonio's fleet was victorious, a description of the event is lacking, perhaps censored by Spanish historians. There followed a stand-off, with the opposing fleets in sight of each other, until the next day, the 25th, which was, ominously for Don Antonio, the Saint's day of St. James, Santiago, the warrior saint and national saint of Spain. However, all too confident of a repeated success, Don Antonio took some of the fleet south-east, intending to take the island of Madeira.

Filipo di Strozzi, Marshal of France

On the 25th, on the outset of the renewed battle off Ponta Delgada at San Miguel, Di Strozzi observed that the wind was changing, which would have put his ships at a disadvantage, so he signalled to Count Brissac to attack without delay, while Di Strozzi's own ship and that of the Count Vimioso pressed the flagship of Santa Cruz very hard. Di Strozzi was met by two Spanish galleons, the *San Martin* and the *San Matteo*, which had come to the rescue of Santa Cruz. Count Brissac attempted to go to help Di Strozzi but due to a contrary wind could not do so. The rest of Don Antonio's navy panicked and fled, leaving Di Strozzi, Vimioso and De Lansac to be taken prisoner, Di Strozzi with a head wound. Under the circumstances Brissac had no option but to follow the retreating fleet back to France.

Despite protests for clemency, Di Strozzi was executed as a pirate the next day. As for Count Vimioso, Walsingham later received a letter from a Dr Hector Nunez that he had received a copy of a confession made by the count, together with his narrative of the actions of Don Antonio in France, which the count had made to Santa Cruz, who was his cousin. This was two hours before he 'died' on 27th July, in other words, two hours before his execution.

After the battle Don Antonio's marshal, the Marquis de Sainte-Soleine, also attempted to leave for France, but Don Antonio had two cannon shots fired at him and so stopped him. "Such had been the disorderly dealing of the French in Don Antonio's cause hitherto," an observer commented.

Walsingham in England who was well-informed on all affairs, described as a very bad man Ascanio Cifarinias, who, he believed, had influenced Sainte-Souleine, persuading him against joining Di Strozzi, so causing Di Strozzi's capture and the defeat of the fleet at San Miguel.

The battle, which became known as the Battle of Ponta Delgada, lasted in total from the 24th to the 27th July. Ships of Don Antonio's fleet that had not fled were destroyed on 26th in the Battle of Terceira, but the main encounter had been that on Santiago's Day, the 25th, when Santa Cruz, with a fleet of ninety-six ships, 9,500 men, and the garrison of San Miguel, defeated Don Antonio's Anglo-French fleet.

As news reached mainland Europe the stories were inevitably confused. The news of the victory by Santa Cruz reached Lisbon where it was welcomed, probably with more than a touch of relief, by the Spanish. They heard that that the French fleet had been scattered like chaff and had been almost entirely destroyed, that Di Strozzi was dead and Don Antonio had barely escaped. The news of the rout of Don Antonio's fleet was confirmed in Spain with slight variations. Di Strozzi was supposed to be dead in captivity and Don Antonio was supposed to be at Terceira. Philip was greatly relieved at this, because the outcome had by no means been certain.

In Paris on 23rd August King Henry had been awaiting news of Don Antonio's success against the Spanish before declaring himself against Spain, but then came unconfirmed reports that he had been defeated. There were hopes that the news was only a fabrication put about by Ambassador Mendoza in England, and Catherine the Queen Mother spoke optimistically about Don Antonio being victorious. In Antwerp it was heard that, although the first fight with Di Strozzi had been lost, in the second, four days later on the 27th, Don Antonio had regrouped and defeated the Spaniards with the help of forces from Terceira and San Miguel, that "King Philip's fleet was wholly defeated," that Don Antonio "remains master of the sea" in possession of the isles of Terceira and San Miguel, but this story was hardly believed. It was only after two weeks of suspense that confirmation was received. On hearing it the Queen Mother burst into tears.

Among the recriminations there were discussions about "failure of loyalty." There was a report that Don Antonio lost ten ships, his fleet had been broken up and he himself had fled from the site of the battle back to the Azores. But another account had it that he had taken San Miguel with the loss of Count Brissac in a bloody victory, and had taken some Spanish ships. But even now Philip could still not take Terceira, it was too strong. Di Strozzi's secretary confirmed the fact that only four ships of Don Antonio had fought the Spaniards and that six in all were taken by them.

Spanish casualties were 553 wounded and 224 killed. They sneered at Don Antonio's fleet for being adventurers who were bent only on plundering fleets and taking possession of the islands, in particular San Miguel. The punishment ordered for the twenty-eight captured nobles and fifty-two knights for their "robberies and piracies" was by beheading in the Piazza, and all the others, all the soldiers and sailors above seventeen years old, numbering 313 in all, were executed by hanging on the same day, 1st August. Nevertheless, the Spanish were of the opinion that this was only a setback for Don Antonio, that Elizabeth still favoured him, and forty ships were to be raised by private individuals in England, while in the Azores there were still about 8,000 Portuguese soldiers and 1,200 French and English.

As if in confirmation of Don Antonio's still-strong position, some merchant ships arrived at Flushing on 23rd September *en route* from Newfoundland. They had called in to San Miguel and Terceira on 4th September, and received assurance that Don Antonio was alive and well and accompanied by forty or fifty good fighting ships of the French navy, that were "peaceable possessors of the isle, and (they) saw many Spanish ships which they had taken." The loss Don Antonio had suffered at the hands of the Spaniards was very small, in spite of the reports lately published, and this consolidation had been possible after receiving reinforcements that had arrived only after Di Strozzi's capture and execution. If this account is true, it is an example of how history is written by the victors, in this case the Spanish, who diminish what appears to have been a Spanish withdrawal without Santa Cruz having achieved his aim, leaving Don Antonio still in firm control.

Declarations of support from the Low Countries for Don Antonio, and his commissions in France against Philip came too late. There were morale-boosting stories in circulation of a victory Don Antonio and the great wealth he had acquired in capturing the Spanish fleet from the Indies, but few believed them. The notion that the battle was only a setback was confirmed as ships in Flanders were being made ready for the service of Don Antonio, in the hope of Queen Mother Catherine providing more.

While the Queen Mother openly supported Don Antonio, King Henry was active covertly, already planning a new expedition. This second fleet was being paid for by the dues imposed by Don Antonio's letters of marque, but the preparations which lasted through the autumn proceeded very slowly due to lack of sailors. Although Don Antonio had no ready money in France he had some in Terceira, where there were already thirty ships and 2,500 French soldiers. Troops were being raised in France, and 7,000 arquebuses and pikes were being collected to arm Portugal.

Don Antonio still had a great many jewels in France to help fund his cause. One diamond alone, that the Duke of Epernon brought to Richlieu, the king's provost, Don Antonio had mortgaged for 45,000 crowns before his departure.

And yet Don Antonio was writing from the Azores, again to Walsingham, complaining to him of the ill luck that he had to report to Elizabeth. But he need not have worried, for Elizabeth assured him of her active assistance, she was persuading ship owners to prepare a fleet that included forty privately-owned ships. The opinion was that if Don Antonio had been better prepared then the outcome of the Battle of Ponta Delgada would have been different. There had been ten or twelve ships ready in England which, if they had been allowed to sail, would have made all the difference.

On 11th October Don Antonio, with Elizabeth's complicity, started from Terceira with between twenty-six and twenty-nine well-found ships and 5,000 soldiers, consisting of 3,000 Portuguese and 2,000 French, on an expedition to take Madeira. But ill-luck struck once more and after being hit by storms fourteen of the ships were lost and so he had to return.

On 11th November an English ship arrived at Southampton from Terceira with news that Don Antonio and fifty Portuguese had been assessing the situation among the other islands of the Azores. Among the passengers who disembarked were five Jesuits who had been found guilty of high treason against Don Antonio, and owing to his magnanimous nature he did not have them beheaded, instead he had them banished and made them promise to go to Madeira with him. But unknown to him they had persuaded or bribed the English ship captains to bring them to England, where Mendoza requested a warrant for them to travel safely to Spain.

King Philip had by no means given up his intention to take the Azores. In a new scheme he hoped to capture Don Antonio and gain Terceira by betrayal, but the plot was discovered. The plan was for the assassination of Don Antonio by the traitor Duarte de Castro, but he was caught, beheaded and quartered along with four others.

In collecting together his reserves, Don Antonio received 60,000 crowns via Lisbon from sources in Spain. Then there was a story, perhaps a subterfuge, that Don Antonio was expected to travel to Antwerp, but instead he collected all the gold and silver he could on Terceira and took it to France, first to Belle Isle and then to Ancenis on the River Loire, twenty miles north east of Nantes. His agent at the French court arranged for him to travel secretly to meet their majesties, as a result of which he had private meetings with the Catherine the Queen Mother.

A small ship arrived in Spain from Terceira with news that on his departure, Don Antonio had left only 600 French in occupation and they were full of an infectious sickness with ten or eleven dying each day, that the people on the island were weary of the Frenchmen's insolence and abuse towards them, and that there was little money on the island other than what Don Antonio had minted, that his gold coins were only coloured gold, with 2/3 copper, and the silver with 2/3 brass.

However, whether this was true or false, the Spanish court heard to its satisfaction that their French majesties "seem not to be well contented with Don Antonio's return from the Terceiras." It was believed in Spain that Don Antonio, accompanied only by his agent Diego de Botelho, was living in "a mean lodging," not far from the Queen Mother's house and that he wished "to cast himself down at Her Majesty's feet" in order to request relief.

The Spanish considered Don Antonio to have been injured "by the violent force of a mightier person," King Philip of Spain, and that he was prepared to make an offer to Philip, to surrender his supposed right and claim to Portugal if in return Philip would allow him to establish himself unmolested in the Azores.

1583
The Azores – Part 2

King Philip in line with his policy of not antagonising the people of Portugal and to demonstrate that he was a benign ruler who respected their interests, had negotiated with Ahmad al-Mansur of Morocco for the return the body of King Sebastian. In early January the Duke of Medina Sedonia crossed the Strait to Morocco to bring the body back to Philip's Portuguese court "to be solemnly buried in the chapel of the Kings of Portugal."

Also during January the story circulating in November was confirmed, that Don Antonio had gone to France where he was secretly living in Paris in lodgings of the Abate di Guadagni, near the Queen Mother's house. Was this the mean lodging that the Spanish would have people believe? He was living in a retired manner where he had been visited by King Henry, who was preparing another fleet for him. Catherine the Queen Mother, his most ardent supporter, had taken Don Antonio under her protection, promising that she would help with ships when Don Antonio himself was in a position to raise a fleet.

From across the Channel, Queen Elizabeth asked how she could help, and offered ten ships. Don Antonio was believed to have 100,000 dollars in France, partly in money and partly in jewels, which was brought to him in ships coming from India. King Henry bought a diamond from him for 70,000 crowns. But despite the goodwill, bad intent was never far away. He was continually, and rightly, suspicious; he accused certain Frenchmen of having been bought by Spanish gold.

The Battle of Ponta Delgada, Terceira

His household, the Portuguese court in exile, was being swelled by Portuguese fleeing to him from Lisbon and elsewhere, to the total of forty of more, including gentlemen it was noted. He had made a claim for jewels held by a Jew in Paris that had been held in trust for many years on behalf of his grandfather, King Manuel of Portugal, but without much prospect of success. The Jew claimed that no one but the Queen Mother had the right to them.

Philip's son Prince Diego, his heir to the throne of Portugal, died on 21st November 1582, so he appointed his nephew, 23 year-old Cardinal-Archduke Albert, the son of his brother-in-law, the Duke of Alva, to rule in his stead as viceroy for Portugal and its empire, then he left Portugal for Spain after two years residence taking "some of the best gentlemen" with him as insurance that there would be fewer nobles to lead any insurrection. About the same time the English were aware that there was an Italian who was dealing underhand in seeking to make an arrangement between Don Antonio and Philip.

Don Antonio sent a request to Elizabeth *via* Walsingham for 2,000 men, but she could not do it without demonstrating open hostility to Spain. Undeterred he prepared for his departure from Paris to Dieppe where he intended to order his little fleet, which was now being rapidly prepared to go to Terceira. It was planned that by spring he would have a fleet of eighty vessels, comprising forty English ships, twelve Flemish and the rest French. For the English participants there was a commercial interest as well as political interest, for there was trade in sugar and wood between England and Terceira.

In the event, 1,500 French departed for Terceira in eight ships. Don Antonio had also requested 300 or 400 English soldiers be recruited because the islanders preferred them to the French, and for another reason that was secret at the time, which was that forty trusted Portuguese were to collect a treasure of 300,000 ducats from the fort on Terceira, and the "money of the fatherless children," a further 115,000 ducats.

Before he left Paris, Don Antonio wrote to Elizabeth, who was in the end to send 1,200 men to Terceira. The island itself was strongly fortified with thirty-two forts and redoubts, a new fort was under construction, and all were well supplied with munitions. There were 1,000 French and English already on the island in addition to the Portuguese.

Elizabeth's agent, Edward Prinn in Rouen, requested 400 or 500 Englishmen to go Terceira to counterbalance the number of Frenchmen. However, on the social side of island life, the French were back in favour and the English were marrying island women.

Further afield, the island of Fogo of the Cape Verde Islands had declared for Don Antonio.

When Don Antonio arrived in Dieppe there was news of support and goodwill from Portugal; more Portuguese nobles were coming to him. Catherine the Queen Mother was getting an army ready for him and King Henry was sending 200,000 crowns "to nourish the war between France and Spain." News from the Atlantic islands was also good; Edward Prinn wrote that on the 14th November the people of the island of San Miguel had risen against the Spanish, killing many and causing the survivors to flee to the safety of the fort.

Don Antonio was supplying the islands with 2,000 men, artillery and munitions; the Cape Verde Islands and Madeira were in his favour; while in France 5,000 foot and seventeen companies had arrived for his service.

In Dieppe Don Antonio his new forces were being assembled including French artillery, with more cannon being founded. In March, when Dr Ruy Lopez arrived in Paris from England, Don Antonio sent word that he wished to speak to him, so Dr Lopez went on to Dieppe with letters from Elizabeth.

More money was due to come from the Portuguese possession of La Mina in present-day Ghana, which was at its height of production during the 16th century, exporting as it did 24,000 ounces of gold each year, equating to a tenth of the world's supply. Sixty Portuguese in two French ships were sent to the fort of La Mina to collect gold to the value of 150,000 crowns.

Don Antonio was at Rouen to mint currency for the Azores, as he had King Henry's permission to do so.

And yet, and yet … things began to go wrong. In Dieppe, Don Antonio was reported to be in misery. Queen Elizabeth, worryingly, had begun to look for ways to improve relations with Spain, and preparation of the second fleet for Terceira was proceeding very slowly through lack of funds. The troops were ready to embark, but the fleet was still fitting out, and it was feared that a Spanish fleet would go to Terceira before it could be got ready. The 1,200 soldiers already in Terceira were suffering from a great shortage of everything; liquids in particular were in short supply on the island. But tension eased when the ships of Don Antonio left the Havre de Grace on their way to the island.

The Dominican friar who had written the book about Don Antonio's just claims to the Portuguese throne on his behalf, returned to Paris from Portugal with two of Don Antonio's natural sons, Manuel, aged fifteen, and Cristobal, aged ten, to the Abbot of Guadagni's house where their father was staying and where he was receiving letters from Portugal.

Two Portuguese came from Portugal, they had a conference with the Queen Mother and departed, but the nature of the conversation was not revealed. In May Don Antonio wrote to inform the Queen Mother that he was at Rueil with his two sons, one of whom was to go to Terceira. At this time there were three vessels getting ready at Honfleur, Normandy, destined either for Don Antonio or, perhaps to keep the Spanish guessing, for Scotland.

Meanwhile Don Antonio's ambassador, Diego de Botelho, who was described as a noble Portuguese, "a person of much wisdom and discretion," arrived in Antwerp on 25th March, bringing letters. Unfortunately, one of his ships had been lost near the port of Sluys and somehow more letters had been discovered on board that had found their way into the hands of Mendoza, who sent them on to King Philip.

The States assured Botelho of their support for Don Antonio's cause and offered him twelve ships with victuals for six months, munitions, and 3,000 men. Then, in anticipation of this help, Don Antonio himself arrived at Dunkirk. He had been very ill but he was recovering, to the extent that he was reported to be able to walk about outside.

But in the end the States proved reluctant to fulfil their offer, so Don Antonio returned incognito in the middle of May to Paris to attempt to obtain further aid, but money at the time was scarce at the French court. However, his troops at last embarked for the Azores, coinciding with the encouraging promise of further assistance from a Spanish defector who offered to work against Philip for the benefit of Don Antonio.

In Constantinople at the other end of the Mediterranean, in June a messenger from Don Antonio arrived at court in the hope of obtaining aid from the Grand Turk, Sultan Murad III, however, there was a truce for the time being between Turkey and Spain, so any action by the Pasha would have to be on Spain's behalf. On the other hand, the Shereef of Fez, Ahmad al-Mansur, was very much hostile towards Spain, but in playing his hand both ways, he had given the Grand Turk the port of Araze (El Araish), which, it was known, had room for a great fleet.

A note was sent from the Grand Vizier of the Sultan's court to Don Antonio assuring him of the Sultan's support, and that if he would send an ambassador with suitable gifts, then the Turks would furnish him with 100 ships, dependent, of course, upon the truce with Spain, a rather slippery offer.

Don Antonio's fleet arrived at Terceira and prepared to meet the fleet of King Philip.

Three ships, probably loaded with munitions, had been captured at Terceira by Manuel de Silva for the cause of Don Antonio. But the seizure was not so simple, merchants arrived in London to protest, however they were assured that Don Antonio would pay for them next year. The fact that the merchants did not complain too much made ambassador and spy master Mendoza consider that it might have been a ruse set up by Walsingham, to make people believe that Queen Elizabeth was not helping Don Antonio. Mendoza thought that those ships went to Terceira specifically with cargoes of munitions.

A Spanish fleet commanded by the Marquis of Santa Cruz arrived at the Spanish-held island of San Miguel to refresh the soldiers he had brought with him, and to embark the men brought there last year, before he set sail for Terceira. By the 19th July he had not yet sailed from San Miguel due to bad weather, but, to his annoyance, this did not stop two or three French ships from attacking any isolated Spanish ships.

The Spanish fleet left San Miguel on 20th July, but for the next two days the wind was contrary and so they did not sight Terceira until favourable weather made it possible. The 23rd, 25th and 26th were spent reconnoitring the island, and a landing was made between the forts on the island on 26th, which augured well for them, since it was the first anniversary of the Battle of Ponta Delgada.

The Spanish troops disembarked on the 28th and took the trenches of the defenders with the loss of twenty men and many wounded. Don Antonio's French troops, under Aymar de Chastes, were routed with the loss of 300. The fleet remained in port and the army occupied the capital city of Angra.

The French fled to the mountains from where they drove cattle and bulls, tied together and deliberately maddened, towards the Spanish, who were familiar with the tactic and simply stood aside to let them pass. They then closed ranks again to attack the French of whom, according to the Spanish report, 800 were killed while the rest fled again to the mountains.

Meanwhile in Spain the people were divided between hopes and fears as they awaited news from the Azores. One Spanish source claimed that Santa Cruz had landed on Terceira, the army had disembarked and had done some slaughter, and that he was making himself master of the island. Although the source of this news was not reliable, another report was that Santa Cruz held the port and chief town and almost all the island; that the French garrison had withdrawn to the mountains where they could not maintain themselves for long.

Don Antonio had his own version of events, declaring that the Spanish force was lost except for twelve ships, that Terceira still held out for him, there the Spanish had been repulsed with about 5,000 killed and that the French, who were ready to lay down their arms, had taken courage at the sight of unexpected support from the little Isla de Fayal (173sq.km./67sq.ml).

But there was no doubt that the Spanish had gained control of Terceira, Don Antonio's stronghold, and Santa Cruz settled governmental affairs with the intention of leaving for Spain on the 17th August.

Santa Cruz granted pardon to the French and embarked 1,500 of them without their arms to return them to Biscay with the exception of four officers, including colonels, who remained as hostages. He also pardoned the islanders, but Manuel de Silva was beheaded on 8th August, and fourteen Portuguese were also executed. The Count de Torres Vedras was beheaded and other Portuguese in his service were hung. Some of the neighbouring islands had intended to resist but on hearing of the defeat of the Azores, they also surrendered.

An English ship returned from San Miguel, where it had been spying in the guise of a merchant. The information it gave claimed that it and another ship had gone to Terceira as soon as the Spanish fleet appeared, to give warning to allow the French ships and others time to get away.

Almost all the Spanish fleet on its return to Cadiz was in need of victuals and medicines for the sick, and more, but no one was allowed on shore. Santa Cruz went to Madrid on 20th August to make his report that twelve French ships had been captured and the French, with the islanders who supported them, had surrendered on the 28th July.

Don Antonio, who had been on Terceira, managed to escape to France, where, at Poissy, he was much displeased by the ease in which the French had surrendered.

Edward Prinn wrote to Walsingham with several items of news: that one of Don Antonio's supporters, Don Juan de Castro, had escaped from Terceira and was in contact with him and Botelho; the anonymous Portuguese friar, the go-between, had been captured and had confessed to Don Antonio's actions in France; and Don Antonio's long-time servant, Juan Rodrigiez de Sousa, had gone over to the Spanish to beg Philip's pardon, asking that he might serve him.

Philip had listened, but before agreeing to anything, demanded that De Sousa tell as much as he could about Don Antonio's plans and secrets. De Sousa must have complied, for he was pardoned and sent to Spain.

Don Antonio wrote from France to General John Norris, commander of the English forces in the Low Countries, admitting to the loss of Terceira. His sympathisers in England expressed their disappointment over the loss of Terceira and the lack of support for him.

In November 1583 Don Antonio was at Rueil, where he regarded himself as safe and still in the favour of Catherine the Queen Mother. He had about eighty people with him, including fourteen or fifteen Portuguese friars, "for consolation in his afflictions," but, supposedly, no-one of quality. He and his entourage were unpopular in the district, provisions were sent to him but the tradesmen were not being paid. A loan was requested of 10,000 crowns but their majesties had none to give. There was no more talk of Don Antonio's cause in France; he had failed.

1584
In France

In January the Spanish ambassador to London, Bernadino Mendoza, was dismissed for his involvement in the Throckmorton Plot against Elizabeth. He went to Paris and he was not replaced. Elizabeth felt obliged to send Sir William Wade as an ambassador to Madrid to explain this action to Philip, but Philip refused to see him and diplomatic relations were terminated.

Don Antonio had his court in exile in France to support, a retinue that now numbered about 120 Portuguese. To his relief, King Henry and Catherine the Queen Mother were once again financing him as well as taking practical action on his behalf; ships were being made ready in his name in Normandy with the intent to annoy the king of Spain. In Antwerp, where rumours abounded, it was heard that Don Antonio had reached an agreement with Philip for a pension of 100,000 crowns and a gift of 200,000. Through his own network of spies Don Antonio was able to give letters to Sir Edward Strafford, Elizabeth's ambassador in Paris, who he thought could be trusted but would soon, in fact, become an agent for Mendoza. The letters concerned had been intercepted on their way from Mendoza in Paris to Alexander Farnese, Duke of Parma, in the Netherlands, but Don Antonio and his agents had been unable to decipher them.

Don Antonio also had his sights set on Queen Elizabeth for help and in January offered to give her a present from the Portuguese crown jewels. This act emboldened him to ask Elizabeth for the use of port facilities in England and a loan of 1,000 crowns per month for six months to buy food and drink for himself and his company. In response, Elizabeth told him that she was willing to allow him into England but could not give him a haven or a place by the sea.

Catherine de Médici, Queen Mother of France

By February the Spanish heard, prematurely as it turned out, that Don Antonio's fleet of seven or eight ships, large and small, with about 2,000 men, was reported to be ready to set sail, furnished for up to a year with provisions and munitions. Its destination was unknown, but the Spanish seemed little worried, their opinion of the Portuguese and French commanders of the fleet was that they were of poor calibre and that Don Antonio's affairs in general were being badly managed.

Hoping to establish a partnership with King Henry and Queen Elizabeth, Don Antonio went to Paris to urge Catherine the Queen Mother to help him but she complained to him of the evil luck they had encountered in all their plans that were intended "for abating the King of Spain's dangerous greatness." Typical of the ill luck was that the departure of his fleet was being delayed from one day to the next. Even so, the French ambassador in distant Constantinople was in secret discussions on behalf of Catherine with the commander of janissaries, the sultan's guard, about Ottoman aid for Don Antonio's cause.

The fleet waited as delay followed delay and by early April Don Antonio was so frustrated by the prevarication that he decided to leave France to go once more to England. Queen Mother Catherine, his greatest ally, was sympathetic and not upset or offended by his decision. As part of the arrangements for his departure he met Sir Edward Strafford, who wrote to Elizabeth that Don Antonio was desperate, that he had had no relief from the King of France, that he was demanding her counsel and wished to warn the queen of a plot against her. To Walsingham, Strafford wrote, "I never saw a poor gentleman whose case I more pity."

Stories that the ships at La Rochelle were destined for Scotland were almost certainly put about deliberately to confuse the Spanish. In July they were even then still preparing to leave when bad luck struck once more and a violent storm sank or disabled the whole fleet. The food and munitions so painstakingly collected had to be thrown overboard and the soldiers were dismissed. All of this took its toll on Don Antonio's health, he was very ill for six days, at first it was thought to be ague but when that left him he remained "in great heat and weakness," seemingly near to death. However, by the end of the month he was past danger and recovering.

All appeared lost for Don Antonio and Catherine tried to reconcile him, "whose fortunes are waning daily," to his fate. She gave him a small castle near Vannes in Brittany and 500 ducats a month. But, comforting as it was, at that time he was full of debt and had to live in hired lodgings in Paris.

Don Antonio was still determined to go to England but felt he could not leave for fear of being murdered *en route* by Spanish agents, so in October it was arranged for his ambassador, Diego de Bothelo, to visit Elizabeth to inform her of his affairs. Around that time there were favourable rumours that King Philip was dead and the nobles of Portugal were wishing for Don Antonio's return.

In spite of his ill luck, Don Antonio was still reckoned in England as someone to be counted upon, along with King Henry of France and the Bishop of Boulogne, for his assistance in the war in the Low Countries. Walsingham believed that Henry would help Don Antonio's cause if Catherine also gave her help. Schemes were devised as to how Don Antonio could be persuaded to "offend and occupy" King Philip in order to distract him from the Low Countries. To assist this aim, the Dutch States General passed acts granting Don Antonio the use of the ports of Sluys and Ostend and giving him authority to detain and hold any ships with goods bound for Spain. This enabled Don Antonio to issue his marque, the licence for armed vessels to capture the enemy's merchant shipping, with the proclamation that, "whatever ships pass into Spanish dominions without safe conduct from himself or his ambassador here, Don Diego de Bothelo, may be taken as lawful prize."

To round off the year, in December Elizabeth sent 7,000 troops under the command of her favourite, the Earl of Leicester, to the Low Countries. The English hostility towards Spain was now out in the open.

1585
The Great Caribbean Raid

Elizabeth had been forced to show her hand. She was helping the Dutch, the rebels in the Low Countries, as fellow Protestants, in their fight against Spain. The most outward political demonstration of this came on 19th August 1585 with the signing of the Treaty of Nonsuch, whereby Elizabeth offered troops and cavalry and financial support in return for the ports of Brill and Flushing. After the assassination of William of Orange on 10th July the previous year, instead of mercenaries and volunteers, English aid was now sent openly. The 5,000 foot and 1,000 horse sent under the Earl of Leicester, against Alexander Farnese, Duke of Parma, proved a distraction but achieved little due to Leicester's incompetent leadership.

Englishmen had served in the Low Countries since 1572, and after 1585, when Leicester went over, were never less than 6,000 men, in addition to those serving the Dutch republic. The experience served as a training ground for English soldiers. Employment with queen of England was preferable because the Dutch were notoriously bad at paying wages. This meant that the Netherlands were a great drain on Elizabeth's finances, but if Spain were allowed to conquer and rule them unmolested then the next target would be England with its heretic queen, as she was regarded by the Spanish.

In March Walsingham wrote to Strafford, the English ambassador in Paris, expressing Queen Elizabeth's wish that King Henry would assist in Low Countries and continue to act in the restitution of Don Antonio. Walsingham strongly suspected Strafford of being a spy on behalf of King Philip, because he was known to have received money from Mendoza. Don Antonio wrote to Walsingham, assuring him of his gratitude and friendship and requesting a passport for Diego Bothelo, his ambassador in the Low Countries, who had earlier gone in fear of being arrested.

Don Antonio had become part of the English scheme to strengthen the Low Countries in their rebellion against Spain, he asserted his assumed authority as king of Portugal with Spain as the enemy. He had armed vessels at Sluys which cruised about with his letters of marque, by which he granted permission that merchant ships bound for Spain could be captured as prizes. With his name and licence a very valuable merchant vessel had already taken that had been en route for Spain. But this circumstance led to complications.

In March Captain William Fenner, Edward Fenner and John Challice, were questioned about ships taken or detained by them in their galleon *Fenner,* by the commission of Don Antonio, and the next month Dr Ruy Lopez, now Don Antonio's ambassador in England, was examined over a captured ship, the *San Francisco,* in Southampton. There was also a question of priority of authority, should Dr Lopez or the ambassador of the King of France, be the person responsible while Don Antonio was still resident in France? The situation was very delicate, for while Elizabeth did not wish to upset Philip too much, at the same time there were English merchants clamouring for compensation from Spain for goods lost to them in Portugal on the overthrow of Don Antonio almost five years before.

There came a distraction from events in Europe. Thousands of miles away across the Atlantic, the Spanish island of San Tomas in the West Indies, all thirty-two square miles of it, had had its discontent fuelled with aid in the form of ships from Don Antonio, and in March a fleet was being got ready in England to support the rebellion. Francis Drake was to be in command, and he was rumoured to be going not with Elizabeth's commission but Don Antonio's.

Disturbances during May in Paris, where Don Antonio was resident, led him to consider leaving for England, but his movements were being monitored and reported to King Philip by a member of his own household who was close to him and known to him as Antonio Escobar; however he was known to a small circle as 'Sampson,' a spy in the pay of Spanish ambassador Mendoza. That Don Antonio was still a cause of concern to King Philip was evident when, that same month, Philip to buy him off by offering him a substantial income on condition that he lived in Italy. On the other hand his fears of plots by King Philip for his capture, or worse, were justified when, in July, Edward Prinn, now Don Antonio's agent in Brittany, met four Portuguese who had escaped from the castle of Boucesa, and heard their story.

There had been an attempt to capture Don Antonio by some Frenchmen sent by the Duke of Mercoeur, governor of Brittany and a Spanish sympathiser, but their intended victim had left three days before. However, Diego Botelho, his ambassador, and his youngest son, 12-year-old Cristobal, were in the castle. In order to attempt an escape, they both faked illness and were taken prisoner to be put in the hands of a Madam la Grenache. However, she freed them and they were able to go to La Rochelle with Don Antonio. Then in August there came news of an imminent assassination attempt, of which Don Antonio was given word only two hours beforehand and was able to escape.

Bernardino de Mendoza, Spanish Ambassador and spymaster

There were references in the intercepted correspondence of Ambassador Mendoza to a Captain Duarte Pachecio, who had offered to do some great deed, presumably Don Antonio's murder. But thankfully for him, he had servants who believed that, although he was now a poor man, one day he would be better situated, so they affirmed their loyalty and were on guard against Spanish plots.

In England, Walsingham was reminded to ask Elizabeth to write, as she had promised, to people favourable to Don Antonio's cause as a proof he was in her favour. The Spanish feared, with justification, that Don Antonio might go to Constantinople to ask for help from Sultan Murad, and a diamond merchant called Alvaro Mendez, who had supported Don Antonio in France, went to the Sultan's court at Constantinople to negotiate on behalf of Queen Elizabeth. There he changed his name to Salomon Ibn Yaish.

Catherine the Queen Mother did what she could, she sent 6,000 crowns to Don Antonio in La Rochelle, she also promised to restore his pension and offered him a safe house. But Don Antonio was not in France, four English ships had brought an embassy to the Prince of Bearn in south west France bordering the Basque country, and he had returned to England with them. This action displeased many French, especially the Queen Mother.

In England, Don Antonio went to live the manor house of Osterley Park in Isleworth, west of London, which had been built as recently as 1576 by the late banker and financier, Sir Thomas Gresham, who had died in 1579.

The fleet for the West Indies, for the commission of Don Antonio, was gathering at Plymouth, and getting larger with Elizabeth's blessing. Great surprise was expressed at the speed with which Elizabeth had made up her mind and committed so much so quickly. This was the fleet that Don Antonio had hoped for, in September he was rumoured to have gone on board with Drake and they were due to sail from Plymouth on either 18th or the 21st. Accounts of the composition of the fleet varied between seven large ships with twenty-two smaller ones, and thirty-five, or forty-four ships, or even sixty-two good ships, carrying seven thousand, or eight thousand, or ten thousand infantry, 500 horse and 200 gentlemen, with the aim of landing in Portugal or the Azores.

An alternative plan was also circulating, that if Don Antonio were to go with Drake they would sail to the Portuguese colony of Brazil. When word of the expedition reached Catherine in France she was offended because, after all the help she had given Don Antonio, she had not been told of this, but she had the good grace to say that she hoped that the expedition would be successful.

Departure was imminent but, as was often the case, due to bad weather it was delayed until the 25th. Unfortunately this gave Elizabeth time to change her fickle mind. Now she did not wish Don Antonio to go with Drake and scoffed greatly at the idea. She believed Drake could not yet have sailed, so she sent a courier to command them both to return to court in London, but too late, the fleet had already sailed on the voyage that became famous in history as Drake's Great Caribbean Raid, taking Drake but leaving Don Antonio, who had been thwarted once more.

However, Drake did take time to sail along the Atlantic coast of Spain to the port of Vigo, which he duly raided and where he re-victualled and did a great deal of damage. In doing so he incidentally encouraged the hopes of the Portuguese. But it was also here that the ill-discipline and rapacity of the men under his command foreshadowed what would happen four years later in 1589.

News of Drake's departure reached the Spanish court in the form of a rumour that he was heading to Brazil with sixty ships, 7,000 infantry and 500 gentlemen. It was also rumoured that Don Antonio was in command of another sixty ships that might possibly join Drake's fleet in the Canary Islands. This story quickly changed to Drake having thirty-two ships and galleons and many transports and brigantines rowing vessels, etc. Then there was uncertainty as to whether Don Antonio would sail with Drake or if he would attack Portugal, in which case defensive action was planned. In the end Drake had sailed with twenty-one ships and 1,800 soldiers, but he was still expected to sack the Atlantic islands on his way to South America.

The Spanish perspective of the expedition placed greater prominence on the role of Don Antonio, they believed him to be a greater threat to their control of Portugal and more influential than he actually was. The Portuguese people loved Don Antonio, whom they believed to be their natural king, and they hated the Spaniards. But the Spanish, to their relief, realised that Don Antonio was not with Drake, that he had been recalled by Elizabeth at the last minute. Even so, he was known to be sending letters in cipher to Portuguese officers to persuade them to join his cause.

The Spaniards hoped to vanquish English fleet which was full of warlike soldiers that had set out, as they believed, in the name of Don Antonio and Portugal, as easily as they had done to the French in the Azores in 1582 and 1583. And yet, perhaps to avoid engendering greater hostility, in May Philip permitted two English merchants in Lisbon, Peter Freare and Bernard Lewis, to trade in certain goods to and from England.

There but for fortune, alongside Drake could have been Don Antonio, the man who would be king of Portugal, but by Elizabeth's command he had had to remain in England, his departure had been false news. He was now staying with Sir Philip Sydney at Buckland Abbey, Drake's house near Plymouth. Drake had betrayed them both. Sir Philip had been the instigator of the expedition, intending to go with Drake as joint commander, and Don Antonio to be among the leaders.

But this plan had created a situation that went against Drake's natural preference for complete control. He informed on Sir Philip to Queen Elizabeth, and whether it was to remove him from the scene or to reward him in some way, Elizabeth instructed Sir Philip to accompany the Earl of Leicester to the Netherlands, where he met his death in war in October the following year.

Don Antonio's feelings towards Drake can only be guessed as he travelled slowly back to London, lodging at the houses of various gentlemen on the way. Perhaps as compensation Elizabeth treated her guest (or was it her captive?) well, she ordered two houses to be put ready for his reception, one of which was Somerset House, but this was only gall to Don Antonio, who could hardly support them unless his pension from the French treasury continued. He had requested 500 crowns, but instead King Henry had revoked the pension while Catherine, until now Don Antonio's main and most consistent mentor, wished him to return to France.

While he was at house nine miles from London, Don Antonio received the French ambassador. This was a diplomatic gaffe that caused Elizabeth resentment; the ambassador should have spoken to her first. However, she did see him on four occasions after he reached to London to stay in the house of Dr Ruy Lopez, who had become Don Antonio's ambassador and was acting as intermediary between them. By her nature Elizabeth was not generous, so she gave Don Antonio just enough money to keep his entourage, his court in exile, in a basic manner, which meant that his people were to be seen about town dressed in London cloth and "fed on beef and beer without any other entertainment."

At the end of the year 1585 encouragement from Portugal came to sustain Don Antonio; he was assured that he was still beloved, that two out of three people were devoted to him and that the country was only a drain on King Philip. However, this was most likely to be information that the informants wished him to hear rather than a factual report, nevertheless it was music to Don Antonio's ears.

1586

Spies and More Promises

Don Antonio sought to repair the breach between himself and the French royal household. He begged pardon from King Henry and Catherine the Queen Mother for disobeying them by coming to England. Henry's attitude towards him mellowed and he ordered 1,000 crowns to be paid to Don Antonio for two months' pension, the money to be taken to him in England from France by a group of friars. Just as with Elizabeth, for their own purposes, Henry and Catherine wished to encourage Don Antonio and to hold on to him, but they would give no sign of active practical support, and in the event, of the promised 1000 crowns, only 100 were raised.

It was reported of Don Antonio's life in England that Queen Elizabeth "caresses and makes much of him" giving him 1,000 or 2,000 crowns at a time. Certainly at Christmas she had presented his sons, Don Manuel and Don Christopher, now aged eighteen and thirteen, with a great quantity of silk and cloth of gold.

In May Elizabeth generously gave Don Antonio 3,000 crowns to pay off his debts and granted him an annual pension of 8,000 crowns. His potential usefulness was again becoming recognised as tension between England and Spain grew and so he had to be encouraged to stay in England. Elizabeth was very much inclined to help him with resources and ships, and although this aroused jealousy in Paris, Henry and Catherine applauded Elizabeth and encouraged Don Antonio with their hopes for his success.

Walsingham, hoping to take advantage of the moment, advised Don Antonio that he should make an alliance with Ahmad al-Mansur in Morocco, but it was not until 1589 that this suggestion was taken up.

Don Antonio was offered four ships towards a fleet that was to plunder Spanish shipping and go on to Brazil, the complete fleet of seven ships was being got ready at Norwich. Ostensibly these ships were merchantmen but in reality they were for the enterprise and Don Antonio was to sail with them. The fleet, that include one ship of 60 tons belonging to Don Antonio to guide them, was due set sail in May.

Nevertheless, Don Antonio in London was prone to bouts of despondency, and with good cause given his previous experiences of Elizabeth's promises. The ships destined for Brazil had not left by 20th July even though they were ready to sail, and, as often was his case, he was in need of money. He complained openly of this to the German ambassador who commiserated with his ill fortune.

Now that Don Antonio's eldest son, Manuel the Prince of Portugal, was 18 years old, he was beginning to take an active role in his father's affairs. Earlier in the year he had been to Flanders with six men in order to join Robert Dudley, Earl of Leicester, under the pretext of having fled from his father. However, Don Antonio had ordered him to go, with backing from Elizabeth. Edward Prinn, Don Antonio's English secretary and sometime ambassador, was with Manuel, writing letters on his behalf.

Rumours began to circulate, perhaps deliberately to confuse the Spanish spies, firstly that Manuel had been captured in a ship bound for India, and secondly that he had been taken prisoner in Portugal with Bishop of La Guarda when going about the country urging people to rebel. But in fact Manuel remained with Leicester throughout the spring and summer until September, when he was summoned to return to England, "to take some enterprise in hand."

Also in the Low Countries, Don Antonio was having coins minted in readiness for his regaining the throne, or at least for circulation in the Azores. The coiners were counterfeiters who normally worked in secret, and for which crime, under normal circumstances, if they were discovered and arrested, they could be executed. But as Leicester wrote to Burleigh, for their working openly at Goicum on behalf of Don Antonio, they would likely only face prosecution because execution would be dishonourable to Elizabeth. In July a stock-taking note was made of all gold coins in Low Countries including Portuguese.

Throughout the year, as indeed at all times, the correspondence of Don Antonio was being intercepted. In February, King Philip was reassured that Don Antonio's letters to Walsingham via his secretary were not alarming, but tension mounted as the year went on. In June Philip granted an audience to a Portuguese woman who revealed that she and others were spies for Don Antonio with a commission to kill King Philip. It could have been this that led to the arrest at about the same time of another Portuguese woman who confessed nothing, but the Spanish were certain she was a spy.

There were of course plots on the Spanish side. In August Mendoza informed Philip from Paris that if a certain plot to kill Elizabeth succeeded, the English would arrest Don Antonio and his people and they would be put in the Tower. But Philip replied to Mendoza instructing him to seize Don Antonio and "serve him like the rest," in other words kill him. The plot concerned was the Babington Plot, which was duly foiled with the discovery of the involvement of Mary Queen of Scots that resulted in her trial on 25th October.

In autumn, Philip wrote to Mendoza introducing Antonio de Vega to him under the name of Luis Fernandez Marchone, with the recommendation that he may be trusted. De Vega, also known as 'David,' went to London ostensibly to join the cause of Don Antonio, to whom he was to refer as 'uncle' in correspondence. In December Philip received a scheme to murder Don Antonio, which he accepted and sent instructions to Mendoza to have it carried out. It failed.

During his time with Don Antonio, De Vega was to make more than one abortive attempt at murder.

Walsingham's network of spies was not only in England. In March, for example, he was informed that there was a Spaniard in Italy who might prove useful to Elizabeth. Then towards the end of the year a Frenchman, John Bolleau, was arrested with his servants, who under examination denied his coming to England with the intent to kill the King of Portugal.

Don Antonio himself did not lag behind with regard to spies. One of his messengers, Lucas Suarez, arrived in England in November disguised as a beggar and three other Portuguese had arrived in France by way of Toulouse.

For King Philip there were three chronic foreign problems, Portugal, the Low Countries and the Ottoman Empire. Don Antonio was a constant thorn in his side, it was through him that Elizabeth had influence in Portugal, and the aid which Elizabeth was giving to the Low Countries gave strength and encouragement to the Dutch, making them difficult to control. From the other end of the Mediterranean, Turkey, Spain's maritime rival and enemy, although now in decline was sending galleys to raid along the coast of the Spanish mainland. In one raid they boldly sailed by Barcelona sacking every ship they could find. Then, to add to Philip's troubles, in early summer his ill health recurred and he was being purged by his physicians.

Elizabeth was growing weary of the course of events, the support for the Low Countries was draining her financial resources and the problem of her cousin Mary had sickened her at heart, so she began to make tentative approaches to come to some sort of terms with Philip.

This alarmed Don Antonio, who was relying on Elizabeth for help to regain the Portuguese crown that he had held for those precious weeks in 1580. To remind her of this, and to impress on her his title to the Portuguese throne, he had had a book written of all the arguments in his favour for the recovery of Portugal that he had wished to dedicate to her.

Francis Drake, Don Antonio's fickle friend, arrived back in England from the Caribbean Raid on 22nd July. It had been a failure; the investors made a loss instead of the anticipated fabulous wealth such as had been brought by Drake's circumnavigation of the globe. There was not even enough money to pay off the 1,000 or so men who had returned alive and Drake had to beg Burleigh for money to settle the bill. As it turned out for Don Antonio, it had been to his advantage that he had not accompanied Drake on the voyage, he had not been tarnished by its failure or by any association with it.

Antonio de Escobar, known as 'Sampson,' the Spanish spy, watched Drake's return. In his report of the event to Mendoza he added that Don Antonio was hinting of fresh activity at sea, a possible landing on the coast of Portugal where people were known to be very discontented with Spanish rule and where there were only 2,000 Spaniards in control. But 'Sampson' added the proviso that he believed that these were lies, only put about to encourage Don Antonio's people. Even so, Don Antonio wrote to King Henry of France and Catherine the Queen Mother to ask if they would help him once more to go to the aid of Portugal.

Despite his ignominy, Drake shamelessly wasted no time in seeking support for a voyage to assist "the King of Portugal, Don Antonio, or on some other service." He was a constant visitor to Don Antonio, offering him encouragement, but, one suspects, for his own reasons. For instance, knowing that Don Antonio was pliable and had the queen's ear, Drake, as an inducement to Elizabeth, wished him to recommend that John Hawkins set out with a fleet, first for the coast of France and then to the island of San Miguel to await two Spanish ships expected from the East Indies.

King Henry III of France

The Spanish court heard that Elizabeth was raising a great fleet of twenty to twenty-five ships, being fitted out for Drake to return to the Indies, and that she had Don Antonio with her. But the fleet so far in fact numbered only seven. The news that Don Antonio would arrive with Drake's fleet had also reached Portugal, where it was received with the inevitable great joy. Indications were that the populace in Portugal, where the feeling for Don Antonio had been growing stronger, would be ready to rise. Many Spaniards believed that Philip should have been more rigorous in his treatment of the Portuguese – the same as he had been in suppressing the Low Countries. There was also a belief that England would come to Don Antonio's aid to take Portugal, and that Spain, to forestall this, should start to think of invading and taking England.

Don Antonio, who was living near Windsor in a former monastery that is now Eton College, was promised money by Walsingham. On 28th October he met the full council at the Lord Treasurer's house in London in a meeting that lasted for one and a half hours. He insisted that Elizabeth had promised funds from Drake's plunder to enable him to take a fleet to Portugal, but as for himself he did not have enough money even to maintain the Portuguese supporters, his court in exile, that he had with him. A list of his household included forty-eight names, and Elizabeth advised him, rather cynically, not to keep so many that he could not feed them. On 3rd November, when Elizabeth sent money and reinforcements for Leicester in the Low Countries, she included a message to ask the Dutch for aid for Don Antonio. In that same month Drake himself went to Holland to get ships fitted out for Don Antonio's cause.

'Sampson' reported to Mendoza that although Don Antonio gave the appearance of being satisfied in England, he believed that this was artifice, so, through him, the Spanish believed that Don Antonio was dissatisfied with Elizabeth after all.

This belief turned out to be true, for in December Don Antonio, in his frustration, requested a decision from Elizabeth either to support him or else to grant passports to allow him and all his people to leave England. He went so far as to arrange with the French ambassador for passports but then he fell ill. This action forced Elizabeth to send him assurances that she would indeed help him. In reply he wrote assuring her that if he appeared off coast of Portugal with a fleet, 8,000 men would immediately join him.

Leicester and Walsingham encouraged Elizabeth to take this opportunity and she responded, very generously for her, by advancing Don Antonio three years of his pension of £2,000 per year and 18,000 crowns, four of her own ships, five of the largest merchantmen in the country, and two smaller ones. Drake visited Don Antonio, swearing that he would place him on the throne of Portugal or die in the attempt.

On his recovery, Don Antonio went with Drake to see his fleet of seven ships, the largest of which was 400 tons, the next was 300 tons, another was 250 tons, and the rest varied between 150 to 180 tons, and all were well-armed. Elizabeth in addition promised something more ambitious that was not quite within her power to fulfil, that thirty armed flyboats and canal boats from Holland and Zeeland would join him, with the possible addition of Huguenot ships.

Nevertheless, the rebel states in the Low Countries had actually offered forty ships to put Don Antonio on the throne of Portugal or, if not there, then in the Azores.

1587
Betrayed Once More

When Mary Queen of Scots was beheaded on the 8th February, King Philip of Spain, as the champion of Catholicism in Europe, could not allow this execution of a Catholic queen to go unavenged and his plan for an invasion of England gathered momentum. But this unparalleled execution, a drastic event of international significance, did not affect the affairs of Don Antonio, the man who would be King of Portugal.

At the beginning of the year a total of sixty vessels were being prepared by Drake, ostensibly for Don Antonio's expedition to Lisbon that would set him on the throne. But unknown to, and perhaps unsuspected by Don Antonio, yet almost inevitably, Drake had his own plans, once again Don Antonio was about to be used a dupe.

Don Antonio's main failing it seems was his trust in English promises. Even though he was referred to, officially at least in court circles, as the King of Portugal, he was being continually exploited. Although there was genuine sympathy for him in some quarters, Walsingham wrote that, "the poor king's weakness of judgement, for lack of experience, has made him enter into jealousies against some of his best affected servants." These jealousies, or suspicions, were not without foundation since at one time or another five spies of King Philip were keeping watch on Don Antonio, and he knew it.

Perhaps Leicester saw the flaw in the Lisbon plan and suggested to Elizabeth that a smaller, less ambitious alternative might be achieved more easily. He pressed her to let Don Antonio go to occupy the Azores, those strategically very well situated islands, with thirty English ships and thirty of the Netherlands. The idea that Don Antonio might go with Drake to the Azores must have been discussed, for the story got back to Spain where it was given credence. At the same time the Spaniards had been informed that, as ever, Don Antonio was short of money and in debt.

All the time, between England, Spain and Portugal, via France, the espionage network was buzzing with activity and rumours abounded. A friar spying for Don Antonio in Portugal was arrested carrying letters to Don Antonio urging him to come to Portugal as soon as possible. The friar was taken to Spain where he was imprisoned for life, and perhaps on the strength of the correspondence, preparations were made to prevent a landing by him. Mendoza in Paris was making payments to Lord Edward Stafford, Elizabeth's ambassador there, who was perpetually short of money, and who, in return, supplied accurate information to Mendoza while sending misinformation back to England.

Philip had at least one messenger, Montesinos, in Portugal in his pay, while in England Antonio de Vega, alias 'David,' the Portuguese spy attached to Don Antonio, who referred to him in correspondence as 'uncle,' sent a coded letter to Philip, stating that he wished to murder Don Antonio but his letter was stopped, probably by Walsingham's web of counter espionage.

Philip at one point wished to have all Don Antonio's servants poisoned by putting something in their beer, which could easily have been arranged, but the main target, Don Antonio, would not fall victim because he took his drink separately. However, it was known that he regularly visited a certain countess where the deed might be done. Another alternative would be to upset his coach or his river boat *en route* to court, and a man had been found who was ready to do it. But Don Antonio was aware of De Vega's double-dealing, he knew him to be an agent of Philip, and that he had won Dr Lopez over to Philip's service, so he plotted to have him killed.

Curiously, it was reported in Spain around this time that Sir Walter Raleigh was offering his services to Philip against Don Antonio, and would send a large supply ship of his own, heavily armed, to Lisbon and sell it to Philip for 5,000 crowns.

In April Don Antonio was still in England and still in financial need, with no indication as to a date for the departure of the fleet. He was not on board ship, although it had previously been believed that he would go with the fleet in person. Since the intention of the expedition was to place him on the Portuguese throne it seems odd that Don Antonio's intended presence should ever have been in doubt. But instead he had been at court in despair as ever with Elizabeth, and pressing her for a decision about his fleet.

He was told that twelve merchant ships, which were to take 12,000 men, were being equipped and would be ready by the end of the month, with supplies for one year. The fleet was in fact slowly being made ready but the Dutch had not come forward with ships, so the number of English ships had to be increased to make up the deficit. Elizabeth requested that the London merchants lend Don Antonio £30,000, which would be guaranteed by her, and to provide him with 3,000 men and a fleet.

Don Antonio might not, after all, have been as trusting as he seemed, because he arranged safeguards for himself. He wrote to the Duke de Joyeuse in France asking him to keep him in good grace with King Henry because the English were prevaricating. Elizabeth was putting him off from week to week, although she had given him 2,000 crowns per quarter, his debts in England were 15,000, and she kept him present at court often enough to prevent his escape. However, contrary to the notion that Don Antonio intended to leave for France, there was still the possibility that he might sail with Drake and go on to the Azores.

Then he received the assurance that, as of the 11th March, fifteen merchantmen with victuals for four months were to be ready to set sail in mid-April. However, he was still very dissatisfied and said as much to one of his agents, Dr Ruy Lopez, about whom ambassador Mendoza said was "a great friend of my informants." It was Lopez who gave out that Don Antonio was in despair of aid from Elizabeth, that he was almost starving, and yet Elizabeth wanted to hold onto him and not let him go to France.

Drake and the fleet with thirty-four ships and 2,000 men set sail on the 2nd April, with instructions to attack the ports where the Spanish fleet was being assembled, to intercept supplies, and take any treasure ships he might come across. The promise to Don Antonio for his restoration to the throne of Portugal, and any recognition of the efforts that he had contributed in raising the fleet had disappeared. Drake, it would seem, did not wish Don Antonio to accompany him and Don Antonio, oddly enough, had raised no objections, perhaps he was not in a position to do so.

An exaggerated report of Drake's departure reached King Philip, according to which he had left with forty well-armed ships and 5,000 men with another forty or fifty ships to join him at Falmouth. This escapade was to become known famously as the "singeing the King of Spain's beard." Once again the involvement of Don Antonio in the inception of such a significant expedition commanded by Drake receives no mention in the history books.

Later in the month Don Antonio was seen to be openly in breach with Elizabeth, and that he wished to sail for Holland, but in secret he requested that a ship be put ready to sail to the coast of North Africa. Wherever his intended destination, from his house in Stepney, which was then a mile from London, Don Antonio was preparing to leave England. He and his supporters had been granted passports to go to France, and Paris was reported to be waiting to welcome him, even though his own followers there were supposed to be dissatisfied with him. On Elizabeth's advice he had dismissed all his followers except for fifteen persons, who eventually had amounted to more than eighty. Then to keep him on her string, Elizabeth began to pay him attention and gave him 6,000 crowns.

Nevertheless, Don Antonio prepared for his departure; he sent a request to France for 20,000 crowns and a castle, and in order to acquire a fleet of his own, or at least one not controlled by Elizabeth or Drake, he sent his eldest son, Manuel, to Holland, reportedly to seek aid in ships and money. To the Spanish, however, Antonio de Vega reported that Don Antonio was starving in an inn, which was not the case, and this raises doubts about 'David.' Was he a triple agent, ostensibly in the cause of Don Antonio, spying for King Philip, yet feeding Philip false reports, and that his supposed plot to have Don Antonio killed was a only ruse to obtain credibility?

In June Don Antonio informed Elizabeth in secret that he had been summoned to Portugal and needed 2,000 men. He was not believed but, all the same, Elizabeth asked him to await her decision pending the results of Drake's expedition. Was Don Antonio testing Elizabeth's fickle support for him?

During most of 1587 King Philip was assembling a great fleet for an expedition against England to be launched that year, and the Duke of Parma in the Low Countries was gathering an army in readiness. In April, Drake, having "singed the king of Spain's beard" at Cadiz by sinking and disabling thirty Spanish ships, sailed back around Cape St. Vincent at the south-western corner of the Iberian peninsular, to arrive within sight of Lisbon, with its well protected port and difficult entrance, which was to be an important factor two years later. He judged that his force was too weak to attack, so he rode at anchor at his leisure as an insult to Spain before finally sailing off to the Azores where he captured the *San Felipe*, King Philip's own ship, an East Indiaman with a cargo of fabulous wealth.

Apart from this prize, Drake's main achievement was that he had burnt 10,000 tons of shipping and caused the Spanish Armada to be put off until the following year. However, his return to England met with a mixed response. The common people in England hero-worshipped him, but his deeds and his disobedience were brought into question, even though Queen Elizabeth had benefitted by £40,000.

When Drake met Don Antonio on 29th July, he was reported to be understandably very obsequious. He made the excuse that he had deliberately sailed by Lisbon with the view to reconnoitre the situation in preparation for Don Antonio's own expedition, even though that expedition as first planned had just been completed. In France, Catherine the Queen Mother believed that if Don Antonio had been with Drake and had entered Lisbon, the city would have risen for him. In Spain Drake's action had only served to sound the alarm, and the potential for surprise, the key element to success, had had its edge taken off. King Philip was forewarned.

In September Don Antonio had business with Walsingham, he was preparing an expedition of his own and had sixteen ships ready, but with his dogged bad luck, he had fallen gravely ill with colic on 13th and was in danger of his life. At the time he was living at a house in London given to him by the Earl of Leicester, who was party to this plan and whose task it was to keep the peace publicly by denying that the ships were for Don Antonio.

As ever, Don Antonio was short of cash, he had not received a penny from the *San Felipe*, the great treasure ship from India taken by Drake on the expedition that had been intended for him, and which, had he been given his entitlement of 300,000 crowns, would have been enough to equip an expedition to Portugal. As a sop, the exchequer made a payment of £1,000 to "King Antonio" towards his debts from Lady Day, the 25th March, to Michaelmas, the 29th September.

Still keeping his hopes of a fleet alive, Don Antonio summoned Diego Botelho, his agent in Holland, to England to discuss the matter, but they were forced to acknowledge that there was no hope in either country of armaments for his cause.

In his correspondence with France, in his dealings with Elizabeth, and in his aspirations for his own expedition, the pessimistic side of Don Antonio's nature was understandably revealed. In May he was rumoured to have written to King Philip, telling him he was prepared to make the ultimate sacrifice by asking pardon from Philip in return for the submission of his claim to the Portuguese throne, and negotiating for the withdrawal of his claim on same terms as Duchess of Braganza. In reply Philip demanded that he make his submission in public.

This possible submission was still being discussed in Don Antonio's correspondence in autumn.

At the age of sixty, King Philip, who was often in poor health, was reported to be physically a pitiable figure, with painful, sometimes disabling, gout and a cataract in one eye, and furthermore, worryingly for himself and for Spain, his heir, Prince Philip, was only eight years old.

Throughout 1587, even without modern communication, news could sometimes travel fast. As early as February at the eastern end of the Mediterranean, the Capadun Pasha, or Grand Admiral, of the Turkish navy had been asking the Venetian and French ambassadors at the Spanish court for information about the Armada that was to be sent against England. The ruler of the Ottoman Empire, Sultan Murad, viewed Spain as having grown too powerful after its acquisition of Portugal and he therefore might wish to annoy Philip. The Spanish sneeringly put it about that Don Antonio had offered Portugal as a fiefdom of the Ottoman Empire if he was given help by Turkey.

There was a rumour that Don Antonio had gone in person secretly to the Barbary coast, then part of Sultan Murad's empire. The Venetian ambassador to Spain, who was about as an impartial source of information as possible for those times, heard news from London that Don Antonio had left London for Constantinople on board a man-of-war, "Some say he will go by sea others by land," he wrote. Elizabeth added strength to the rumour when her ambassador was instructed to put pressure on Murad not to enter a truce with Spain. As a gesture of goodwill, she offered to return the Turks who had been captured on board Spanish ships by Drake while he was in the Canary Islands.

Although he did not in fact go to Constantinople himself, Don Antonio had sent a spy, or agent, called Alvaro Mendez. Disguised as a Jew and signing himself 'Solomon,' Mendez claimed credit for himself in saying that King Philip's truce with Turkey would have been successfully concluded but for his intervention. But Mendez was under observation by Philip's spies. Later in the year in Constantinople, the Capadun Pasha entered into discussions with Mendez, news of which reached the Pope, who became concerned that possible co-operation between Sultan Murad and Don Antonio might lead to a revolt in Portugal. In fact the sultan had refused Don Antonio's request for money but he had promised to send his fleet during the next year. The Turkish navy at the time totalled around 300 vessels.

In 1587 France was distracted from the cause of Don Antonio by a civil war involving the monarchy, King Henry of Navarre and the family of Guise. As the year was drawing to a close, Don Antonio was in England, and because of his close links with the French monarchy he was called upon for help. King Henry of France asked him to negotiate with Elizabeth on his behalf to make peace between the two countries over negotiations with Huguenots for the supply of 4,000 men. Such a request enhanced Don Antonio's status both between the monarchs and in his presence at court, but he was indiscreet and was soon in a controversy for expressing his opinions.

Meanwhile in Portugal espionage was rife, several spies of Queen Elizabeth and Don Antonio had been arrested, the Spanish occupation was a continual source of discontent, and disaffection was growing daily. Edward Morys, a correspondent of Burghley, wrote to him from Dover to inform him that among the intelligence from the continent was the opinion that Don Antonio "might easily be restored to his throne."

1588
The Invincible Armada

Philip's wish for Spain was that when he died his son Prince Philip would come into quiet possession of Spain and its empire of the Low Countries, the Indies and Portugal. However, as things stood, with continual trouble in Holland and the presence of Queen Elizabeth's forces, with English ships continually endangering his fleet, and Don Antonio in England fomenting trouble in Portugal, this was unlikely to happen.

The looming war with England met with no enthusiasm in Portugal, the population had no desire for conflict with England, the country which harboured Don Antonio with his, and their, hopes to rescue Portugal from Spanish control with English assistance. From intercepted letters the Spanish were acutely aware of strong indications that Portuguese of high rank now wished for Don Antonio's return. Philip at last acknowledged that his advisers had been right, that he could not win the Portuguese people over by kindness, and so he agreed to repress them by coercion and force.

In London, after two days of talks with Queen Elizabeth, Don Antonio was still uncertain as to what to do. He wished to leave England but that would be difficult to achieve without Elizabeth's knowledge. Catherine the Queen Mother wanted him to send his sons, Manuel and Cristobal, to France. He wrote to Paris that Drake and Admiral Howard would put to sea but didn't know when, and he also understood from Elizabeth, to his great concern, that she desired peace with Spain at any price.

From King Philip's point of view, it was in his interests to keep Don Antonio in England and so attempted to disrupt his planned departure from England by instructing his agents to tell him stories of the dangers that awaited him in France. He instructed Mendoza to subtly suggest to Elizabeth through his channels the inadvisability of letting Don Antonio go.

One possibility, an excuse for Don Antonio to leave, was that Sultan Murad, the Grand Turk, wished to meet him in person. Mendoza's spy, 'Sampson,' was opening Don Antonio's letters to Constantinople which revealed that, if he could escape, Constantinople would be the place he would go to. Perhaps as camouflage, Don Antonio asked 'Sampson' to request 400 or 500 crowns from Catherine the Queen Mother to help his escape. A rumour was put out that Don Antonio had actually gone to Turkey, being escorted as far as Gibraltar by thirty English ships.

Elizabeth had changed her mind as usual, and was urging Sultan Murad to send his fleet against Spain, promising him 300,000 ducats as an incentive, as a result of which, Turkey looked certain to send a fleet. In Spain it was reported that Elizabeth was said to have sent 500,000 crowns to Constantinople. Don Antonio in his, own interest, had already sent a man to Shereef Ahmad al-Mansur in Morocco.

Don Antonio was determined to leave England, intending to go first to Holland, and he began to put his plan of escape into action. In March he went several times with three or four companions to a pleasure house in Brentford, eight miles from London, where he stayed sometimes for ten or twelve days. But this was only a ruse to get the royal court and Elizabeth used to his absences without telling anyone where he was going and without raising suspicions. However his plan was betrayed to Elizabeth by a Portuguese. Don Antonio had left London for a change of air on 25th March and had carelessly taken a favourite dog with him that was recognised and led to him being caught and arrested near Dover. The news soon reached Philip in Spain.

At court Don Antonio had to plead that his absence had been due to illness; he was excused and all was forgiven. On April 19th he was with Elizabeth once again, who was full of kindness and promises towards him, reassuring him that he was safe in her country and that they were friends. But in Don Antonio's own court all was not well, one of his malcontented gentlemen, Don Juan de Castra, went over to France, and several others of his supporters left his service.

In May there was a rumour that Don Antonio had made peace with Philip and he wished to become Philip's vassal, that he had given up hope, and his attitude was noted as being the "poor spirit and great incapacity of Don Antonio, which makes him unable to restore and preserve himself in power." However, during that same month a fleet was being collected with 7,000 or 8,000 men at Plymouth that had a dual purpose, firstly, to forestall Philip's armada, and secondly, to assist Don Antonio to land in Portugal. 6,000 men had been raised in London, where they were drilling twice a week.

Encouraged by this, Don Antonio, as part of the efforts to raise funds, gave patents to English merchants to trade with Portuguese colony of the River Gambia, as a result of which English traders to the Gambia were able to donate 8,000 cruzados. As he had done before, Drake held meetings in secret with Don Antonio about the fleet setting sail, which it was due to do in about a fortnight. Don Antonio expressed his wish to go with the fleet, with or without permission, or else to retire altogether. To plead his case with Elizabeth, Don Antonio stressed his belief that Portugal was in revolt and Elizabeth promised him that if peace with Spain could not be made then he should go with his fleet, at which he was so delighted that he kissed her garments. The Spaniards were aware of the situation that Elizabeth was planning to send Don Antonio to Portugal with an army in hope that the country would rise. Another small but important indication was that the English ambassador in Portugal was in favour with the people.

In Spain there was fear that the Turkish fleet would descend on some part of the coast, and it was known that spies from Turkey and England were active in Portugal. Then disappointing news for Don Antonio arrived from the eastern end of the Mediterranean. It looked unlikely that the Turkish navy would sail after all, or if it did it would be too late to damage Philip's cause. On the other hand, at Elizabeth's request, it was likely to sail to El Arisch in present-day Egypt to winter there and by doing so intimidate Ahmad al-Mansur, Turkey's enemy, and force his cooperation. Pressure on Morocco came from another quarter. In the Turkish province of Tunis, Hassan Pasha was making great preparations to restore to the throne the son of Muley Maluk, the king who had fallen in battle with King Sebastian of Portugal in 1578.

From Paris, Mendoza wrote to his spies, 'Julio,' 'Sampson,' and 'David,' in Don Antonio's entourage and at court, to do their best to keep Don Antonio in England. 'Julio' was a "new friend," 'Sampson' was Antonio de Escobar, and 'David' was Antonio de Vega, who, unknown to Mendoza, was a triple agent, although all of their loyalties in both directions were questionable. Mendoza was cunning and none of the men knew of each other's existence.

In June 1588, before the Invincible Armada set out, the idea of diverting and dividing Philip's forces as a distraction from the main thrust, by attacking him in Portugal, his own country, in the interests of Don Antonio, was broached by Lord Admiral Howard in a letter to Walsingham. On the 14th June he had written from his ship *The Ark* in Plymouth that he wished "King Anthony had set foot in his own country to give King Philip occupation there."

Elizabeth promised Don Antonio decisively that if the war continued she would use all her forces for his aid and "would miss no opportunity of ruining his enemy and hers." But this had all been said before.

King Philip's Armada of 130 ships, 8,000 seamen and 20,000 soldiers departed from Coruna at the north-west tip of Spain, or the Groyne as it was called by the English, on the 22nd July and it appeared off the Lizard in Cornwall on the 28th.

Admirals Howard, Drake and others had set sail from Plymouth on 1st July with 140 sail and around 8,000 men. Don Antonio had not gone with the fleet which he thought had been gathering for him, because Queen Elizabeth was on the alert again and watching him closely, but she still reassured him with promises and secret supplies of money. However, she sent orders to the admirals of the fleet that they were not to take him if he attempted to join them. Elizabeth's detention of Don Antonio suited King Philip's purpose, but for good measure he instructed Antonio de Vega, 'David,' to cut off all the paths of escape that Don Antonio might think were safe; to assist in this De Vega was entrusted with 500 cruzados.

Elizabeth, who, of all people, was impatient at the delay, was seeking and expecting aid from Turkey. Sultan Murad was still being urged to support Don Antonio, and to do this her ambassador, Harborne, was instructed to tempt him with the promise of plunder from the Spanish empire, that in doing so he would enhance his reputation as a great ruler by reviving the glory of the Ottoman Empire and a protector and restorer of rightful princes such as Don Antonio, who would "assuredly repay His Majesty with greater recompense." Elizabeth entreated Don Antonio to send one of his sons as a pledge to Turkey with 200,000 ducats for Turkish navy. He was also to send letters in secret, but with Walsingham in the know. However, instead of sending Don Antonio's son, it was suggested instead that a man of some account should be sent with jewels as a promise of good faith, to be handed over when the Turkish fleet actually set sail.

Concerning the Portuguese crown jewels, Don Antonio had only one gem left of all those he had brought with him from Portugal, and that was the most valuable of them all, the eighth greatest diamond in the world, which he pledged to a Monsieur de Sancy. Murad finally agreed to send aid to Elizabeth and Don Antonio, but it was to be dependent on the current war with Persia.

Don Antonio was still unhappy at his detention, he was about to escape on a French ship but the Spanish spy network found out and got word of it to Elizabeth, so instead he sent a request to the French consul to furnish him with 2,000 men with aim of going to Portugal. In this scheme Elizabeth was to provide the ships as soon as the remaining ships of the Spanish Armada were well away from Spain. By the 9th August it was evident that the Invincible Armada had failed, in the final reckoning only fifty-three major ships returned to northern Spain, the rest were lost, along with 9,000 men.

The focus of attention now moved to a variation on Howard's proposal to attack Portugal and Spain. This assumed a definite form soon after the flight of the Armada, when, in September, Sir John Norris, nicknamed 'Black Jack' for his dark hair and complexion as well as his temper, presented to Elizabeth a complete and thorough plan for fitting out an expedition with the same objects but funded by means of a joint-stock company, which would be both patriotic and profitable at the same time. This appealed to Elizabeth because the treasury was empty.

Elizabeth was to nominate a treasurer for the whole adventure, and give him the sum of £5000 as surety for her part, with other adventurers to be found who would make up £40,000, the total cost of the enterprise. A memo from Burleigh detailed the proposals for the expedition under Drake and Norris that included 4000 men to be procured from Holland, as well as 2,000 horsemen volunteers. The aims were threefold, at this stage they were:

1. *To attempt to burn ye shippes in Lysbon and Civill* (Sevile).
2. *To tak Lysbon.*
3. *To tak the Ilands* (The Azores).

At the foot of the memorandum Burleigh set down the "Articles of offers from King Antonio." In addition to this there was a general stocktaking after the Armada, including an assessment of the condition of ships and monies for payment.

Either 'David,' or 'Julio,' gave the Spanish false information about Don Antonio and Portugal and the possibility of French assistance, but correctly (and harmlessly) reported that the English fleet was being refitted. Soothingly the spy reported that Don Antonio recognised Philip as a beneficent prince because he had not consented to order him being murdered. Later in the month it was reported that an agent of Don Antonio had departed from Paris with letters from King Henry and the Queen Mother. The informant was 'Julio' and it was a lie. In Paris Mendoza was becoming suspicious about 'Julio,' he noted, "For some time he has told me nothing but fiction."

The supposed proposal for Don Antonio to go to Constantinople was still current, and there was still fear in Spain of the Turkish fleet. Philip wished to negotiate a truce, but this seemed unlikely, because Hassan Pasha in Tunis was known to be hostile towards Spain. The Spanish knew that Elizabeth was reluctant to let Don Antonio go, but Mendoza believed that in private she intended to help him in an attack on Portugal by offering him forty to fifty ships in order to prevent him going to Constantinople. In order to gain the firm friendship of Ahmad al-Mansur Don Antonio intended to send Cristobal, his younger son, to the Moroccan court as a demonstration of good faith. On behalf of Don Antonio, Alvaro Mendez was due to arrive in Turkey, but when he did he felt insulted by the lack of belief in him expressed by the Turks.

In the autumn of 1588 there was great activity in England towards helping Don Antonio. At Westminster Elizabeth formally commissioned Sir John Norris and Sir Francis Drake to take charge of and to direct an enterprise, authorising them to "make choice of officers and to levy troops for the service, to invade and destroy the powers and forces of all such persons as have this last year, with their hostile powers and armadas, sought and attempted the invasion of the realm of England and the dominions of the same." Preparations for fifty ships were being hurried forward, six of them being fitted out in Plymouth and most being fitted out by private individuals in the hope of gaining riches, as from Drake's previous voyages. A great number of bullocks were being slaughtered and salted to provision them.

Noble names were among the adventurers, some of whom were Sir John Burroughs, Sir Roger Williams and Sir Charles Blount. King Henry of Navarre even offered forces for the service of King Antonio. The Spanish spies knew that Don Antonio and Drake had met for two hours one day, and that Don Antonio had confidently given an agent of his an invitation to meet him in Lisbon the next Christmas. But Mendoza was aware that Don Antonio was possibly suspicious of 'Sampson,' and therefore sent a new agent.

In Spain it was believed that if Don Antonio were to sail before Christmas he would probably go to the Atlantic islands of Madeira and the Canaries. In Portugal vigilance increased, a Portuguese was arrested on a charge of conspiring with Don Antonio, and he confessed as much, and a prominent Lisbon merchant was executed for having treasonable relations with Don Antonio.

John Norris wrote to Walsingham to request that her Majesty's ship the *Victory* accompany the expedition to take the King of Portugal, it being a larger ship than the others. Norris also requested licences to buy 6000 quarters of wheat, the same quantity of malt, and licence to transport 3000 quarters of wheat and 2000 tuns beer. Money for the enterprise came flooding in, £10,000 from the City of London, £5,000 from Leaden Hall, Francis Drake personally gave £2,000, Drake's friends gave £6,000, and John Norris and his friends donated £20,000.

With regard to the composition of the fleet, the Queen was to contribute six ships, and the City of London and other towns, twenty good ships. The supply of powder and ordnance was noted, and there a commission was issued for levying 6,000 soldiers. Some troops were to go to Ireland as well, and all the while the reckoning for Invincible Armada was still ongoing. A full estimate of charges for building ships for her Majesty and provision of stores was published. In November Admiral Howard sent a bill to Burghley for payment of £623.10s.11d. for victuals, wine, cider, sugar, etc., that had been supplied to ships at Plymouth. Certificates of powder, shot, stores, etc., from her Majesty's store were issued to ships in the charge of Drake. In addition, 200,000 ducats worth of provisions had been promised from Holland.

To Don Antonio, all of this was being got ready for aiding his cause, but other aims were being added to the list, including the burning of Spanish ships and sailing on to the Spanish Indies. And even now, in November, Elizabeth was still awaiting the final reckoning of the Armada.

Intelligence arrived in England that the Duke of Medina had arrived back in Spain with only fifty ships remaining, and that over eighty of the greatest Spanish ships had been lost. King Philip was furious at the failure, he refused to see the duke and had several officers of the victualling department executed. Nevertheless, the prevailing opinion was that this massive failure was only a setback and that Philip was preparing another fleet of over 150 sail. The boast went about that the Spanish would attack again, but this time not from the Narrow Seas, in other words the English Channel.

Drake saw Don Antonio constantly in secret and claimed he was doing his utmost to obtain aid for him. Sir John Norris had gone to the Low Countries to seek assistance for the expedition in the form of ships and cash. He wrote from Zeeland that troops there were ready to join him. In Paris Mendoza was informed that Don Antonio only knew what Drake and Norris told him, about the numbers of men, the ships and their cost, but that Don Antonio, having been deceived so often, was not sure whether or not to believe it. The fleet might be going to the Indies for all he knew. As well as Drake, John Hawkins was constantly with Don Antonio, who began to grow so confident that he reportedly saw himself already restored to the throne.

It was in November that Don Antonio sent his younger son, Cristobal now fifteen years old, to the city of Fez in Morocco as a measure of trust and good will, because Ahmad al-Mansur had promised him a large sum of money, 250,000 ducats, however, he was not completely confident of this because he believed that the Moors often broke their word. Don Cristobal set sail on the 10th November with four ships, six merchantmen and a large household of Portuguese and English, including household staff and several musicians to while away the time on board as well as to entertain the shereef. His father had spent 30,000 crowns on the envoy. But due to bad weather he was thought to be still in the channel by the 25th.

In fact the weather had been so bad that he had had to return as far as Margate. Don Antonio, who had been at the house of a certain Lady Rich at Gravesend for ten days, was very displeased and very impatient about the matter. One of the entourage, Don Pedro de Valdes, who had spoken ill of Don Antonio, was brought to London to be put in chains.

After setting off a second time, Don Cristobal had to return again due to bad weather, this time to Dartmouth, but he had sailed again on 19th of November. He was soon able to send good news when, on the way to Morocco, three of his fleet had fought a Spanish ship which they forced to withdraw to St. Malo in Brittany. Of Don Cristobal's mission, the Spanish recorded that, "a bastard son of Don Antonio has gone to Africa to bring galleys into Portuguese waters."

For the Spanish there was still doubt as to the destination of Don Antonio's own fleet, was it to go to Terceira in the Azores, or to Portugal? Portugal was confirmed as the likely destination where the people had informed the English of the best places to land a force, in particular near the castle of San Gian at the mouth of the River Tagus.

Supporters of the expedition in England were made aware that they should not to write to Portugal because their correspondence would be opened by agents of Cardinal Archduke Albert, King Philip's governor.

At Rouen 'David' sought King Philip's advice about going to Morocco to find out what Cristobal was doing, or else to go to Don Antonio, as he had urgently requested.

Drake, who had just returned with Colonel John Norris from Bergues, on the border between France and the Low Countries, was ready to embark with Don Antonio, twenty of the queen's ships and as many Dutch, and 7,000 men, to sail to Portugal. On his way Drake intended to touch at Coruna and other places in order to pick off any vessels of the Spanish Armada that, owing to the stormy weather, were very much out of order and, he believed, very carelessly guarded. Norris on the other hand had returned from Holland with doubts that troops could be spared for expedition.

Don Antonio promised to keep King Henry of France and Catherine the Queen Mother informed of progress, because, from past experience, he was still waiting for absolute confirmation that the fleet was for him. In an effort to raise more money, he sent six ships to Guinea in a contract with some English merchants with an ambassador to the king to form an alliance and with hopes of borrowing money.

In Spain the rumour which was a fact was circulating that Drake was on the point of sailing with forty ships, had not been confirmed but it was believed, while a firm, unshakeable understanding between Elizabeth and Don Antonio about Portugal was something to be dreaded.

Elizabeth had sent an ambassador to Al-Mansur, which aroused Spanish suspicions. The shereef agreed to march on Cueta, Tangiers and Asila, ports held by Spain by virtue of its possession of Portugal. Events as they developed were being followed all over Europe. The Venetian ambassador wrote to the Doge:

"We hear that Cueta, a city in Africa belonging to the crown of Portugal, is going to give itself over to the king of Morocco, through the negotiations of the bastard son of Don Antonio, who is in those parts, and of the queen of England's ambassador, who has made the king of Morocco understand that unless he proves himself and open enemy of Spain he may expect a large and powerful Turkish fleet at any minute to arrive from Constantinople to harry his kingdom, and to seize El Arisch, as the Grand Turk is suspicious of him on account of the continual presents he is receiving from Hassan Pasha, and thinks he will one day hand over that port to the King of Spain. Pray God the news be not true, for it would be very serious. I fear it is for the ministers here try to cover it up; some, however, do not absolutely deny it."

Elizabeth instructed Sir Edward Stafford, her ambassador in Paris, to declare that the rumours of aid from the sultan of Turkey and the king of Morocco against the Spanish were untrue.

Elsewhere, Elizabeth had sent spies to Spain who were pretending to be fleeing Catholics. Two friars were being held in the prison of the Inquisition and a nun from Portugal was in a convent awaiting sentence. The nun was believed to be a saint but had proved to be a fraud, induced by the friars to tell the deeply religious Philip that unless he handed Portugal to Don Antonio he would be damned for ever, and that she had the further object of raising the people against the Spanish king.

In late December Philip was accurately informed by his spies in England about the financing of the expedition; that Drake was to contribute 12,000 crowns, the Earl of Essex 10,000, Norris 8,000, and London merchants 24,000, while the queen had personally advanced 20,000. Elizabeth received an estimate of whole cost of the army and proportion of ordnance. Her subscription ultimately reached £20,000, besides seven ships of the Royal Navy. Directions were issued to levy 250 soldiers and 65 pioneers in Essex, and 100 soldiers and 25 pioneers in Hertfordshire, to be embarked at London on 25th January. Promises of arms and money were forthcoming in abundance, and flocks of idlers high and low, offered their valuable services.

It was evident from letters of Don Antonio's friends in London that it was not until the end of December that he was completely confident that this time the fleet was really intended for him and his cause. Finally, the terms of agreement for what was to be the English Armada was announced by Queen Elizabeth on 31st December 1588, the clauses read as follows:-

First her Majesty the Queen of England undertakes to provide a fleet of one hundred and twenty vessels and twenty thousand men—15,000 soldiers and 5,000 sailors—with captains for both services, to go and restore Don Antonio to the throne of Portugal.

Don Antonio undertakes that within eight days from arrival of the said fleet in Portugal the whole country will submit to him in accordance with the letters he has received from the principal people in the said kingdom.

Item, That on arriving in Lisbon the city will be reduced at once without any defence and all Castilians in it killed and destroyed, and, for the friendship and aid thus shown him in recovering his kingdom, he undertakes to fulfil the following things – namely:-

First that within two months of his arrival in Lisbon he will hand to her Majesty the Queen as an aid to the costs of the fleet five millions in gold.

Item, In testimony of the help she has given him he will pay every year to the queen for ever three hundred thousand ducat in gold, placed and paid in London at his cost.

Item, That the English should have full liberty to trade and travel in Portugal and the Portuguese Indies and the Portuguese equal freedom in England.

Item, That if the queen should not desire to fit out a fleet against the king of Spain in England she shall be at liberty to do so in Lisbon and shall be helped in all that may be necessary.

Item, That the castles of San Gian, Torre de Belem, Capariza, Oton, Sao Felipe, Oporto, Coimbra and the other Portuguese fortresses shall be perpetually occupied by English soldiers paid at the cost of Don Antonio.

Item, That there shall be perpetual peace between her Majesty the Queen and Don Antonio and they shall mutually help each other on all occasions without excuse of any sort.

Item, That all the Bishoprics and Archbishoprics shall be filled by English Catholics and the Archbishopric of Lisbon shall be at once filled by the appointment of Monsieur de la Torques.

Item, On arriving at Lisbon every infantryman shall receive twelve months pay, and three extra, as a present from Don Antonio and they shall be allowed to sack the city for twelve days, on condition that no man of any rank shall presume to harm any Portuguese or molest the churches or houses wherein maidens are dwelling; and also that they pay in money for whatever they may need in the country.

Either Queen Elizabeth had driven a very hard bargain, or else Don Antonio had been unbelievably naïve in his desperation to become king. By blindly giving away everything he would simply be a client, a puppet of Elizabeth, and Portugal would be forever in debt to England. What would the people of Portugal think of their king when they woke up to the fact that their Catholic country had been saved by Protestants, to whom they would be forever subservient? And that

English Catholics, who Elizabeth had sometimes treated unmercifully, were to take over the highest position of the Portuguese church.

And as to money, 5,000,000 ducats to be paid in gold in the space of only two months, and 300,000 paid to England every year, on top of the cost of maintaining the English occupation of the forts, where was that all to come from? By this agreement, assuming that the restoration was successful, Don Antonio, as King Antonio of Portugal, would be giving away his country. England gained everything, and when the Spanish learned of these conditions they were shocked, they believed that Portugal was governed by Spain on terms more sympathetic and generous than those laid down here by the country's would-be saviours.

In the meantime, it was thought that the fleet would sail at the end of January.

Part 2
1589

Preparations

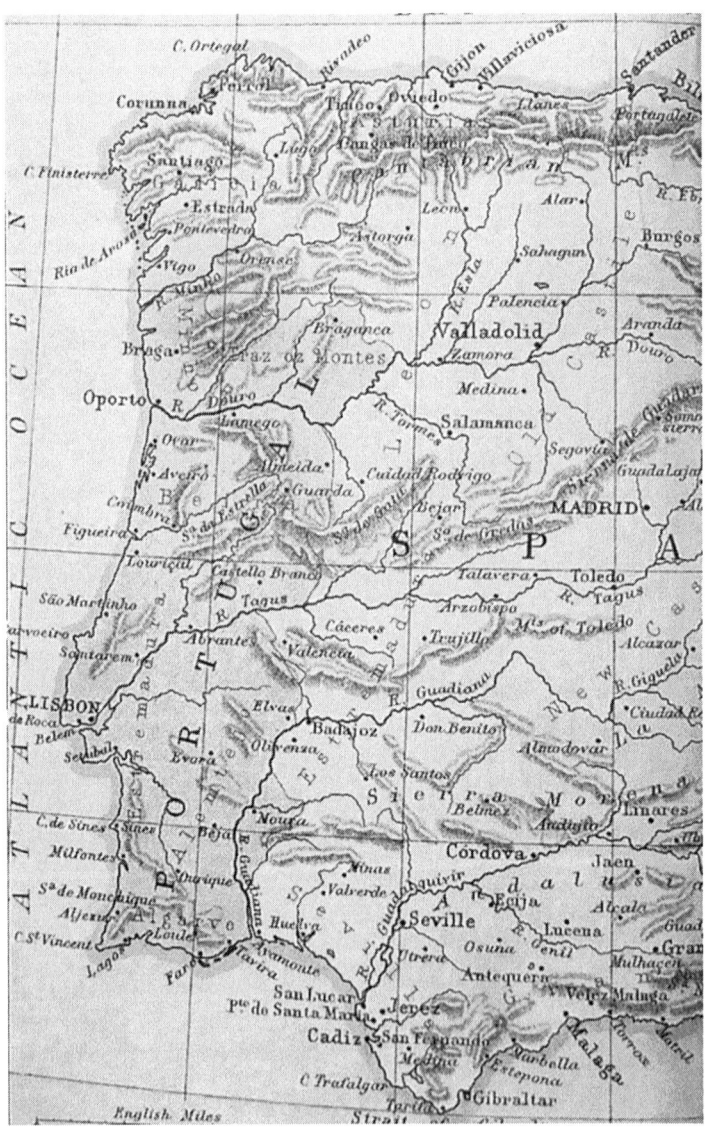

Portugal and western Spain

In January 1589 preparations for the expedition were gathering momentum. Towns and cities were rushing to make their contribution in anticipation of rewards on the return of the enterprise. For example, the townsmen of Ipswich sent two hoys (small vessels rigged as sloops for short distances), for service with the fleet: Soldiers and pioneers to prepare the way for the army from Hertfordshire were ordered to be in London by 20th of the month: Gloucester and Tewkesbury were to contribute a ship and a pinnace (a ship's boat, either eight-oared or schooner-rigged), to the fleet: In the Essex a proportion of the county's rating was to be collected as pay for the soldiers and pioneers: On the 21st all Portuguese prisoners from the Invincible Armada were released on condition that they went with Don Antonio's fleet.

Elizabeth had been sending small amounts of money to the Low Countries, with small detachments of troops, enough to needle Philip, because the Low Countries were seen to be nothing but a drain on the resources of Spain, maintained by Philip only out of duty and his believed right of inheritance. English troops that had been mustered for service there were diverted for the Portuguese enterprise, which resulted in the weakening of forces for the Dutch cause. Rumours spread in the Low Countries, perhaps spread intentionally to confuse the Spanish, that a great army had already left England with Don Antonio as its general.

In its administration Elizabeth's government had to be flexible yet firm, for example, the licence for collection of wheat to feed the troops was extended, while a careful note was kept of money spent by Drake and Norris on provisions and munitions, etc. Until all was ready, the muster of soldiers and pioneers was deferred to 1st February, and additions were made to a new law for punishment for desertion. Meanwhile across in France, Mendoza was being kept up to date with the progress by his spies close to the English court.

As part of the planning, a Captain Whorwood set sail to for the coast of Spain with instructions to obtain information on Spanish preparations for war. His ships were soon sighted by the Spanish off Cape Finisterre, and on his return the news he brought was of naval activity and the manufacture of ordnance in Lisbon in fear and readiness for an invasion of Madeira by Drake, the Spaniards were still unsure of the aims of this English Armada. Whorwood's news led to a request that the supply of cordage, the ropes for rigging, be speeded up.

As a caution, Al-Mansur in Morocco was warned that if he did not declare himself to be an enemy of Spain, then a Turkish fleet was likely to arrive from

Constantinople to harass his kingdom and to seize the city of El Arisch in present-day Egypt for fear of it being handed over to Spain.

The governor of Ceuta, a Portuguese possession on the north African side of the Straits of Gibraltar, through negotiations by Don Antonio's son Cristobal, had had successful talks with Al-Mansur, about handing the city over to Don Antonio and Elizabeth. The talks were relayed to Henry Roberts, Elizabeth's ambassador to Al-Mansur's court, who returned to London from Fez on 12th January. In Fez, Roberts had made a request for 300,000 crowns and the shereef was apparently ready to lend Don Antonio 10,000 crowns, or 150,000 ducats, and provide a fleet to distract the Spaniards from Portugal in order to defend Andalucia. Roberts was accompanied by his opposite number from Morocco, Merzouk-Rais, who was met by Elizabeth, and received by her, and by Don Antonio, as an ambassador. The London merchants also showed an interest in him.

For part of the arrangement, as a demonstration of good faith, Don Cristobal was to be left in Morocco as a hostage. Elizabeth sent her thanks to Al-Mansur for showing favour to Don Antonio at her request and expressed mutual good will. Across the Straits in Spain it was known Elizabeth was in negotiation with Al-Mansur, and that it had been arranged that when she sent her fleet the shereef was to advance against Cueta, Tangiers and Asilah along the North African coast. This led to Spanish counter measures being taken, although they were unspecified.

The fleet was getting ready, if it were to sail at the end of January it was rumoured that it would go to the Azores to leave Don Antonio there with 3,000 men, then go on to the West Indies. As it happened, when the 1st of February arrived, the date originally planned for setting out, nothing was ready, but there was an army of idlers who wanted to be fed, and months later, when the fleet finally was ready to sail, it was found that most of the ships' stores had been consumed to the point that some of them had not a week's provisions left. Money began to run short and Drake and Norris wrote daily to ask for more.

Early in February an inventory of the composition of expedition was made; the fleet of ships and their captains, the numbers of mariners, and the names of the merchant ships. Forty-nine vessels were ready in the River Thames. The fleet included Sir John Hawkins' own ship *The Repentance,* to be commanded by Sir Martin Frobisher, for the service of which money was due to Sir John, and two flagships that belonged to Drake, *The Revenge* of 500 tons, and another, the *Sans*

Pareil of 700 tons. Notes were also made of the composition of the army, all its stores, its munitions and powder.

A list of names was made of officers who were to command the regiments that were to be embarked at London, Southampton and Plymouth. Part of the army consisted of veterans from the Low Countries. An estimate was received from Drake of the cost of provisions already made and yet to be made for the fleet, and the same was received for arms and munitions by Norris, commander of the army. They were reimbursed within a couple of days.

The fleet should have been ready to leave on either the 14th or 15th of February, but concern was expressed that the ships could carry only 12,000 men, while 3,000 men remained unprovided for in victuals and arms. In view of this, on the 15th Elizabeth summoned Parliament to raise money for the expedition.

On 23rd of February the Queen Elizabeth gave her formal commission for command of the enterprise to Sir Francis Drake and Sir John Norris, and issued the warrant of her instructions for the expedition, with its three purposes, now refined to:

1. *To distress the King of Spain's ships.*
2. *To gain possession of at least some of the islands of the Azores in order to intercept Spanish ships to and from East and West indies.*
3. *To assist King Don Antonio to recover the Kingdom of Portugal if the public were in favour of him. Don Antonio to be left in Portugal while fleet proceeded to the Indies.*

There was also a safeguard in the secret appointment of Sir Roger Williams and Thomas Fenner as successors to Drake and Norris should anything happen to them.

Elizabeth gave her authority to issue warrants to adventurers for their shares and assurance that if expedition was delayed by her own orders she would pay the whole expense. The country was aflame with enthusiasm, "Courtiers and swashbucklers touted their hardest for subscriptions to this joint stock warfare, and pressure was put upon country gentlemen to subscribe liberally as a proof of their patriotism," a pressure not to be disregarded in those doubtful times. She wished for trade with Spain to be suspended until after the expedition. Don Antonio was not referred to, although he responded to the articles to Drake and

Norris. His promise to reimburse the adventurers and to pay the soldiers of the enterprise was noted.

By the end of the month all the ships and the army were collected together and ready to sail, except for four ships that were due from Bristol. The names of the generals, estimates of tonnages of ships and the names of their captains had all been confirmed. While all the time the assembled soldiers and mariners required feeding. On the 26th February bills came from the cities of Dover, Canterbury, Winchester and Southampton and the County of Kent for feeding the soldiers and the supplying of ships up to their departure from Plymouth.

During all the month of March and, as it turned out, the first two weeks in April, while waiting for favourable conditions to sail, commanders Drake and Norris wrote heartrending letters to the Council and to Walsingham. The provisions had run out, they said, the enterprise would fail if help was not sent at once. So far the cost had been £51,188 14s. 8d. The army had been detained at Plymouth more than fifteen days and since the taking of fly boats it had almost doubled in size, which, although it pleased Drake and Norris, meant that much of the stores had been used to sustain the men and so they had to request more.

Drake and Norris reported that the fleet had been delayed because of adverse winds. It had already left harbour once but then the wind had changed, so it had had to put back. The remaining stock, it was estimated, would last a month, and in fact the supplies would run out before the fleet sailed, which would incur, as they stressed, dishonour and disgrace to England and Her Majesty and all the adventurers if such a lame ending were allowed to be the conclusion of the expedition, and they repeatedly begged for more provisions. Then on a cheerful note they added that army was in excellent order and, by arrangement with the mayor of Plymouth, fresh supplies were to be sent after them with all speed from Plymouth once they had set sail. The commanders hoped to get relief after their arrival in Spain, although Drake pointed out that "20,000 persons are not satisfied by small means," inferring that supplies had to be sent in sufficient quantity if the army were unable to live off the land.

With the delay of the departure of the fleet, its composition was once again reviewed and it got ready to sail once more on 14th March. Then on the 19th Norris said that he could not ship the troops in less than twenty-five days.

Outside of England, circumstances continued to auger well. In Spain, despite Mendoza's best efforts at espionage from Paris, there were still doubts as to the destination or purpose of the English Armada; would it go to Portugal or to the

Azores, or await Spanish developments and then generally obstruct Spanish movements at sea? In March Drake wrote to Walsingham informing him that he had detained many boats with cargoes of pitch and masts that were on their way to supply the Duke of Parma in the Netherlands, and that he was waiting for more munitions from the Low Countries. In the Azores there had been a rising on the island of Terceira. It was reported from Portugal that the castle of St. Gian near Lisbon had only three or four pieces of artillery remaining with some more in the tower of Belem, the rest having been taken for use in the Armada. Other news came from Portugal that there were very few soldiers in Lisbon, only 150 in the castle and very few in the fortresses.

As for Don Antonio, after all his years of false promises and broken promises, his waiting and his tribulations, as King Antonio the First of Portugal, he was at last preparing to come into his own. His fleet was on the point of sailing, Al-Mansur of Morocco was rumoured to have offered to lend him 10,000 crowns, although his son Don Cristobal, was there as a hostage. Drake, in readiness for his landing in Portugal, had given him 10,000 crowns credit. He had 500 or 600 general pardons printed to give out and he had collected a lot of church plate to take with him to reward the ecclesiastics and to appeal to them. But all the while a member of his entourage, Antonio de Vega, Mendoza's spy with the code name 'David,' was well informed of all this and intercepting all Don Antonio's correspondence.

A possible consequence of this interference might have been that an agent of Don Antonio, Friar Joseph Tejeda, who went to Lyons in February had to flee back to England after an attempt was made to arrest him at a monastery on the accusation of writing books against King Philip. On the 16th March Don Antonio and his eldest son Don Manuel left London for Dover to board ship. Norris and Drake were to be there on the 19th ready to meet him and in expectation of the arrival of a fleet from Holland.

At length, on the 23rd of April 1589 the expedition finally sailed for Plymouth with eighty ships, but even then this was only a feint so that the men might be kept together on board and not stray on shore to get out of hand. As a record showed, "the crosse windes held us two daies after our going out, the generals being wearie thrust to sea in the same wisely chosing rather to attend a change out there than to lose it when it came by having their men on shoare."

On the 25th a fleet of eighty ships set sail again for Plymouth, where, given a fair wind, they expected to arrive on the 28th. Don Antonio was on board Drake's ship and his son Don Manuel was with Norris. Merzouk-Rais the Moroccan ambassador, who was dressed as a Portuguese, sailed with Don Antonio in order to take news of developments as soon as possible to Al-Mansur, who would then send his promised men, arms and money. From Fez, Don Antonio's son Don Cristobal reported that he had been very well received since his arrival at Safi on the western coast of Morocco on the 7th January.

As the fleet passed Rye on the south coast, the spy 'David,' was watching, ready to report to King Philip. He advised Philip that a watch be kept in Portugal at Buarcos and Cintra. He wondered whether to go to Madrid in person to account to King Philip. He also advised that an offer of 1000 cruzados be made for the capture of every man accompanying Don Antonio. 'David' left England early in April to report to Mendoza, and although he was unable to return straightaway, he did so not long afterwards.

Another reason for 'David's departure was that he was being too closely watched by the English court and Don Antonio, who had kept him near so as not to upset the French ambassador. 'David' had many carriers for his messages but it was hoped that he himself could be tricked into embarking on a ship from where he could be thrown into the sea, or at least arrested. On Don Antonio's behalf an agent of his was seeking more money from Jewish lenders.

In Morocco, as March turned into April, the promises made by Al-Mansur were becoming more vague and dilatory. A rumour that he had already supplied gunpowder proved to be false. A possible reason for his vacillation was that two Moroccans of royal blood were in Spain and the shereef therefore did not want to make an enemy of Philip. Alarmed by this, Elizabeth and Don Antonio sent their agent, Edward Perrin, who arrived in Fez on 12th April, and together with Don Cristobal he held successful negotiations with Al-Mansur.

All the same, Perrin was suspicious of the shereef's sincerity; three English merchants had been executed in Morocco for one Spaniard, and other English merchants were being detained. Part of the argument used by Perrin to Al-Mansur was that if the shereef failed to prove himself a true friend of England and Queen Elizabeth, then he could expect a large and powerful Turkish fleet to harass his coast, because, as Al-Mansur well knew, Murad Rey, the Grand Turk, was suspicious of his activities there.

Shortly afterwards, as if in confirmation of English influence in the region, a fleet of twelve English ships passed through the Straits of Gibraltar which was assumed by the Spanish to be on its way to Constantinople with a new English ambassador. They also suspected that if Elizabeth sent a fleet to Portugal, as it was now anticipated, Al-Mansur would attack the places on the North African coast held by Spain by virtue of its possession of Portugal.

At last all of the fleet, this English Armada, was now at Plymouth and ready to sail. As an observer gave thanks, "It has pleased God this day," when on the 6th the wind was good. About this time Drake and Norris heard a rumour, a wild one as it turned out, that that 200 Spanish ships had arrived at the Groyne, as Coruna was called by the English, and other Spanish ports with munitions, cables and other stores, but, undeterred, they reaffirmed their aim to destroy all shipping on the coasts of Galicia and Portugal. Then misfortune struck. During the middle of the month, on the 13th, furious gales began blowing in the Channel, and then, in addition to the lack of the fair wind necessary to set sail, came the report that the fleet was short of victuals and money.

Other ill omens began to appear before the expedition set out as some of the promised support failed to materialise. As many as eight out of the twelve heavy artillery pieces, siege weapons, that had been promised were not delivered, the loss of which was felt soon after landing in Spain and Portugal, when town and city walls had to be attacked. 600 English horse were expected from the Low Countries, and although they were transported at great expense, for some reason not one reached the fleet.

Likewise, only seven of the anticipated thirteen old companies of battle-hardened soldiers from the Low Countries joined, and only four out of the ten Dutch Companies, with six of their promised men-of-war. It was intended that the experienced professional soldiers would improve the overall calibre and level of competence of the army. Then finally there were some of the adventurers and some "divers gallant courtiers," who got cold feet and withheld their investment to the tune of £10,000.

But nevertheless the expedition had been got together. The aspiring fighting men had been cajoled and tempted into the belief that they were going on a great plundering expedition; that they would return home soon, wealthy enough to make them independent for life. But there were serious defects in the army that were never rectified, there were no surgeons and no transports for the wounded and sick; provisions were said to have been shipped on board enough for two months, but in some of the ships the men declared that they were starved from the first day; and from the outset general discipline was slack.

As to the total manpower, on the eve of departure Norris and Drake told the Council officially that the total number of all ranks and sorts was 23,375, but other figures differ. Captain Fenner, Drake's vice-admiral, gave the number as 21,000, Captain Baillie of the *Mary German*, in a letter to Lord Shrewsbury, said that the landsmen alone were 20,000, as Drake had stated. The historian William Camden wrote of only 12,500 soldiers, and another historian, John Speed, put the number of landsmen at 11,000 and mariners at 2,500. From the standpoint of the enemy, Count de Portalegre, one of the Portuguese nobles who had been 'turned', reported to King Philip that the army which arrived at Lisbon, its destination, consisted of 12,000 men, and a Spanish diarist wrote that 16,000 men-at-arms left England and very few sailors.

To gloss over what ended in an abysmal failure, one authority later believed that the "terrible mortality from sickness, &c., and the comparatively small number that came back made English writers of the time anxious to minimise the disaster by underrating the (original) numbers of the expedition." However, the official figure is accepted as being the most reliable.

Of the men-at-arms, all but three or four thousand old soldiers, mostly from the wars in the Netherland, were described by critics as "idle vagabonds whose first idea was loot and whose last was fighting. In addition to these there were 1,200 gentlemen or more, the flotsam and jetsam of the Court, younger sons of slender fortunes, and gallants whose hearts were aflame to do good service to their country."

In the fleet there were seven of Elizabeth's best ships of 300 tons each, twenty other armed ships and a large number of transports and galleys 'of light draft', which was the original complement. In addition to this, sixty small German ships which had been wintering in the Netherlands were pressed into service, adding to the number which finally reached a total of nearly 200 sail. At first only six of the queen's ships had been allocated but when Drake, as Norris had already done, wrote to the Council asking for an additional larger vessel, the *Victory* was commissioned, the reason being "in respect of the King Don Antonio."

The cost of maintenance per man had been set at £24. 6s. 0d. for each foot band and £30 for each horseband, with £280. 16s. 8d. for winter apparel and £187. 19s. 4d. to each foot band, and appropriate credit had been authorised to merchants. Although General Norris had hoped to get many more troops from the Low Countries, Sir Roger Williams claimed he "never saw such willing minds nor such celerity." There were reports of divisions between the men but it was agreed that the army, for the price, was "the best cheap that was ever levied."

This enthusiasm was not shared elsewhere. The innkeepers and victuallers of Canterbury, Southampton, Winchester, Plymouth and other towns wrote to the queen demanding payment for stores they had supplied. The Dutch shipmasters commanding the flyboat transports contributed by the States formally protested and refused to put to sea with such insufficient provisions as they had been given; and then, just as it looked as though the expedition would break down for good, there came providentially into the harbour a Flemish ship with a cargo of dried herrings, and another ship with five hundred pipes of wine, and, above all, a sloop loaded with barley. These provisions were promptly transferred to the fleet to the dismay of the ships' masters, who fruitlessly protested for a long time afterwards against the confiscation of their cargoes. On the 7th, the fleet was finally declared ready for sea, but then came contrary winds that kept them in and out of Plymouth harbour for several more days.

A significant distraction occurred one day while the fleet was waiting to set out, Sir Francis Knollys, a relative of Elizabeth, her "plain-spoken and dependable cousin," and her treasurer, came unexpectedly and post-haste from London asking if anybody seen or heard anything of the Earl of Essex. Drake and Norris had already received letters from Knollys warning them that the Earl of Essex had left the royal court without the permission, and that the queen was in a towering rage at the disobedience of her favourite. Elizabeth ordered the fleet not to sail until he had returned.

The first Earl of Essex, Robert Devereux, was the oldest son of Walter Devereux, who had become the stepson of Robert Dudley, Earl of Leicester when Dudley bigamously married Devereux's widow. At twenty-two years of age the impetuous Essex was Queen Elizabeth's latest pet and he was about £23,000 in debt. He had resolved to steal away with Drake, in the hoping of making his fortune with the expedition, or at least to make enough to pay his debts, and he was perhaps tired of tediously entertaining this old lady, Queen Elizabeth, and of his bickering with Raleigh. He had gone on board the ship the *Swiftsure,* captained by Sir Roger Williams, second in command of expedition, who had sailed off without the commander Drake's permission.

Curiously, nobody in Plymouth reported having seen Essex, even though only the day before a party of young nobles from London had dashed into the town, all dusty and travel-stained, to be welcomed by the couriers and officers of the fleet.

A few hours after Knollys' arrival, when the Earl of Huntingdon came with warrants of arrest and 'all manner of peremptory papers', that included a letter to Drake and Norris commanding them to arrest Williams. Drake saw that the matter was serious both for himself and Norris, because they knew that Williams' ship had put to sea hurriedly and unannounced as soon as Knollys explained his mission. Somehow the word had immediately got through to him.

The commanders' immediate answer to Knollys was to deny all knowledge of the earl's intention to join the fleet, and that same night they sent a pinnace after the *Swiftsure* to find it if possible and to inquire if Essex was on board, and to recall him. However, there was no news of the missing earl and nothing more was seen or heard of the *Swiftsure,* Essex or Williams until much later in the expedition.

While the rest of the fleet was delayed in Plymouth for another ten days waiting for a fair wind, Drake and Norris wrote to Elizabeth nearly every day until they sailed, continuing to deny any knowledge of Essex and his intention to join the force and expressing their deep sorrow. Of course, Elizabeth knew enough and more about intrigue, so she did not believe them, and from that time she had nothing but "hard words and sour looks" for the adventure that had robbed her of her favourite.

The armada finally set sail on the 28th April. It had on board the army of 14,000 men, divided into fourteen regiments of five companies each, consisting, in addition to the English, of Germans, Flemish, Walloons and French. This was only the army, there were, in addition to this, the sailors who served on board and brought the final total of officers and men to 23,375.

The fleet itself reached a total of 125 sail, "mostly small or middle-sized, as is usual in England," the Spanish reported dismissively. Drake, the terror of the Spanish, they knew was in supreme command of the fleet, and Norris, "a man very famous among the English," was to lead the soldiers on landing.

At the last minute there was some disappointment when the Dutch ships refused to depart, the reason their master gave was that they were not supplied for so long a voyage, even though they had agreed with Drake and Norris to serve with them for three months commencing 15th March.

Once out in the Channel the fleet was still delayed by rough sea and bad weather. This was not to the liking of some of the adventurers, who thought they were going to sail "over summer seas to a paradise of plunder," and 3,000 men in twenty-five ships, probably most of them that were owned by the reluctant Dutchmen, deserted. Two companies were lost from on board two ships alone. This desertion to some extent explains the difference between the accounts given of the numbers of the expedition.

At last, on their third day at sea the rest of the fleet caught a fair wind and set off across the Bay of Biscay in fine spring weather, four days later they sighted Cape Finisterre. Provisions were already running out during the week that the ships had been at sea, and complaints of short rations were to be heard on all of them. In this situation, it was judged by the commanders Drake and Norris that the only way to keep the crews from open mutiny was to give them the opportunity to plunder, so instead of obeying Elizabeth's strict instructions to attack the Spanish fleet in port, and to land Don Antonio in the country that he believed was yearning for him, Drake, who was far better at commanding than obeying, sailed instead for Coruna on the north west tip of Spain.

Reactions In Spain

While preparations for the expedition were progressing in England, in Spain the failure of the Armada was still reverberating. Of the 130 ships that had set out from Coruna the year before, only a total of sixty-six returned. Survivors from the fleet went to King Philip to claim their due payment but Philip ordered them, with severe penalties for refusal, to return to the armada that was being repaired in order to set out again. They obeyed their monarch, but very unwillingly.

Spanish propaganda gave out that Spain had not been dismayed by the failure of 1588. In November an Italian report had glossed over the apparent tragedy, almost optimistically claiming that:

"The Spanish Armada has returned to Spain, thanks be to God, after routing Drake several times; he always refused to fight. The cold coming on, the Spanish sailed around England and came home. This first journey will make the Spanish acquainted with those waters, and the attack on England will now be quite easy. Already the Spanish provinces have promised to furnish and maintain fifty thousand men to fight the English, and so your lordship may guess whether the expedition will cause any difficulty or not. Has anyone ever heard of a like offer made by a people to its Sovereign."

Early in January a report reached Madrid that an English fleet had appeared off Santander, however this proved to be false. Philip, however, had other distractions, Catherine de Medici, the Queen Mother of King Henry of France, was suddenly taken ill and she died on the 5th January. This and the death of Henry Duke of Guise led to unrest in France and popular risings in Paris against King Henry. Catherine the Queen Mother had for long been a constant supporter of Don Antonio. At the same time Philip was intriguing to keep the French out of Italy.

On the 23rd King Philip was attacked by a fever which came on again two nights later. He was also suffering from painful gout in one knee. As a result of the treatment for the fever by purging, he was "very feeble and worn in body," and at the age of sixty-three his doctors were anxious for his future, believing this generally to be a dangerous time of life. However, by early February the king was able to get out of his bed each day at midday, but only to sit in a wheelchair because he could not yet walk.

Although Spanish preparations for war were in some quarters dying down in January, and officers of the Cortes were raising difficulties about granting funds, several naval captains were in conference about assembling another Armada, as well as putting together another fleet of thirty ships with 3,000 infantry men and engineers to build forts to be sent to New Spain, the name by which Mexico was then known.

It was estimated that another two months would be needed to make ready fifty guard ships to protect Spanish waters, but Philip was concentrating his attention on events in France, and then there was also fear of an invasion from across the Pyrenees by Henry, the Protestant King of Navarre. In the event the fleet for New Spain did not sail for fear that 'El Draco,' 'The Dragon,' Drake, might be in those waters, as well the fact that, by the time it reached the Caribbean it would be the hot season.

When it came to the construction of new warships, the Spanish had not learned the lesson in modern marine warfare as taught to them by the English the year before. The ships they were building were not the new-style, fast, light, manoeuvrable ships such as those of the English that had proved so effective in the Channel, but the typical floating castle that Spain had always built. The new warfare at sea, evolved by Hawkins, Drake, *et al*, was a method of hit-and-run cannonades from a distance, whereas the Spanish method was to sail close enough to board the enemy ship and then indulge in hand-to-hand fighting.

News that there was fear of an uprising came from across the border in Portugal. In order to suppress it King Philip asked the Cortes for more money and instructed his nobles to hold themselves ready with their men-at-arms to go either to Portugal to quell an insurrection or to Navarre to meet an attack from France. The Cortes relented and granted supplies and a million and a half in gold, which was rather short of the two millions that Philip had requested.

As well as these events in Europe, the Spaniards were very aware that Queen Elizabeth would carry on doing all she could to annoy them. In Fez, Don Cristobal, together with Queen Elizabeth's ambassador, Edward Perrin, was in negotiation with Ahmad al-Mansur, which led to an agreement in March whereby, amongst other things, the shereef would seize the Spanish possessions on the African coast opposite Gibraltar.

English ships were sailing in the waters off Galicia "doing much mischief," and they would have entered the port of Santander to seize the ships being built or repaired there had they not been prevented by a new fort built at the mouth of the harbour. On the 15th they were sighted off Finisterre and news arrived from Lisbon that forty English ships in squadrons of eight and ten had been sighted off the coast of Portugal. The Spanish believed that the ships had "secret relations" with Portugal and feared that they would unite under Drake to attack Portugal, before going to the Azores then on to the Indies.

As tension in Spain increased during February when the twelve English ships passed Gibraltar on their way to Constantinople with a new English ambassador. Venetian merchant ships also came under suspicion. It was decreed that any of them were found to be trading with England and the heretic queen they were to be confiscated. This, together with the constant threat from the English themselves in revenge for the Armada, meant that the situation was such that Venetian ships in the port of Lisbon were afraid to put to sea. There was some justification for Spanish suspicion after all, because certain Venetian merchants had been found to be carrying not only normal trading goods but sulphur, saltpetre and munitions.

The early part of the year saw the delays in preparation for the English fleet, and this apparent lack of activity led Philip to believe that any attack had been cancelled, but nevertheless he still ordered precautionary measures to be taken against it.

At sea there was also the factor that Drake was unpredictable, that he might appear anywhere. Fears of an English attack on recalcitrant Portugal that would bring Don Antonio to the throne were compounded by the activities of Al-Mansur. With regard to Portugal itself, Philip ordered Duke of Albuquerque to be ready with forces on the Portuguese border if Drake should appear, and commanded leading Portuguese nobles of doubtful loyalty, and those known to be disaffected, to come to his court.

Philip's health continued to improve, by the 11th February he was able to walk around his room with a stick, but three days later he suffered a relapse when the gout returned to both feet. Thankfully for the king the relapse proved to be temporary and ten days later he was much better, he was living his usual retired life but he was able to attend to affairs of state. Then towards the end of the month his ten year-old son, Prince Philip, was taken ill with a violent sickness and he was unable to stomach anything. The previous year he had had ulcers on his legs which had closed over and medical opinion was that they might have gone to his stomach. A fever followed and as a last resort a bezoar stone (the gastro-intestinal stone from a goat which, in the middle-ages, was believed to have the power to remove all poisons) was given to him, after which he was able to keep his food down and the fever went.

Even though King Philip was said to be in great distress about his son, he did not visit him and carried on with normal business, it was only when the prince had turned the corner that his father visited him for the first time. A fortunate turn of events for Philip was that France was now in such a disturbed state that even King Henry was not safe, and Spain had no cause to fear an invasion.

In March the English ambassador to France had left to seek help for the French king from King Henry of Navarre. Meanwhile Philip continued to assemble his army, which still might have to be called upon for a purpose other than to repel an invasion of Portugal. There was trouble at home, King Philip was not popular among his people of Catalonia, that is, among the people who counted – the nobility. In order to unify Spain he had attempted to curtail their long-held fueros, or privileges, this was followed by open resistance and protests in the street which actually compelled Philip to back down. But so long as he was feared and obeyed, popularity counted for little with him, the armies he was preparing might not be used only to resist an English attack across the border, they could be used against rebellious subjects.

English corsairs and pirate ships were a continual problem to Spanish commerce. On 29th April a ship sent in advance of the main Spanish fleet from New Spain arrived home two months after the fleet itself, having suffered bad weather and by having to fight off an English ship for five days, and then evading capture by four others. Its eventual arrival was especially welcome as it carried 150,000 crowns.

In the north, two Spanish ships returned to Coruna after being sent to obtain information about the situation on the English coast. They reported, mistakenly, that "although Drake is arming in all haste yet he will not take the sea very early owing to the disturbances in France." On their way back they had taken the opportunity for a small revenge when they seized an English ship and brought it back with them. A witty observer remarked that, in doing so, these two ships had done more than the entire Armada the year before.

Philip's preparations for an anticipated war in Portugal were continued by distributing 2,500 Spanish infantry around the country. And yet despite this, attitudes in general relaxed, for there was the belief that that the Portuguese would not rise, and there was confidence that there would be no danger from Drake even if he did land. In Spanish reports, it was always 'Drake' that was referred to, for he as an individual was regarded as the enemy as much as the nation of England.

On 13th May Philip was ensconced some twenty miles north west of Madrid at the Escorial, the hub of Spain and its empire, to where he had summoned a council of war. The Venetian ambassador to the Spanish court noted that there was criticism throughout Spain of the tardiness of preparations, when it was known that an English fleet was all but ready to set out, but it was happily assumed that the fleet was weak or was bound for somewhere other than the Iberian peninsular.

Against the advice of his doctors Philip was intending to go, with a militia of 6,600 to accompany him, to Valladolid, some one hundred miles from Madrid further to the north-west. This was so that he would be on hand should trouble arise with France and Navarre, as well as to collect the eight millions in gold from Castile, a demand with which Valladolid was refusing to comply. A one-year truce had been made between King Henry of France and King Henry of Navarre that could pose a problem to Philip, given their hostility towards Spain. There was also the threat of the arrival of a Turkish fleet in North African waters and close to Spain. But Philip was confident of dealing with them all.

Preparations continued in Portugal, although not very rapidly given the situation, where the people were believed to be impatient for the arrival of the English who would bring their King Don Antonio. The Portuguese had always resented Philip's rule and were restive, even with the threat of severe penalties and the presence of Spanish soldiers. Philip wished to repress any seditions that might arise in Portugal, so any potential leaders of an uprising in support of Don Antonio were being banished or executed. But there was always the fear that Drake would arrive with an English fleet to encourage rebellion.

The troops with which Philip was filling the garrisons were intended to impress by their sheer numbers rather than their ability. They were inferior in the quality of both horses and men, including as they did even the rawest recruits pressed unwillingly into service, who were "more valuable for their quantity than their quality." A display to impress and cow the Portuguese was all the more necessary because the planned Armada would not be ready until the following year and Portugal was reported to be in "violent and open commotion," awaiting the arrival of Drake, the supernatural bogeyman and the deliverer of their king.

There were indications that offensive action against Spain was imminent. A Portuguese spy of Don Antonio's was arrested in Lisbon, who had come from England on his way to Morocco to speak to Al-Mansur. When questioned, according to him Elizabeth had 400 ships ready to put to sea as was originally proposed, but this was treated as a rumour. There were, however, signs of activity in Fez, and there was the continual fear that the Turkish fleet might still put to sea.

Ahmed Al Mansur, Shereef of Morocco

Curiously, as fear reigned in Philip's council, vigilance in northern Spain, where the English would be likely to attack first, was relaxed due to the perceived delay in the departure of the English fleet and even its possible cancellation. This belief led to a false sense of security and in the event, although the Spanish government was continually on the alert and generally well informed by its network of spies in England, Spain was nevertheless taken by surprise when

Drake suddenly left England with 125 ships. Spain was practically defenceless against a sudden descent on its long coastline, and most defenceless of all was the extremely remote north-west corner of Spain, where Drake had decided to land.

Coruna

To the astonishment of the Spanish, on the 4th May the English fleet appeared off Coruna, a port where it was least expected. At the mouth of the harbour the ships cast anchor, "striking terror into the inhabitants of that city and the surrounding country."

The panic-stricken, yet slow-moving, attention and mobilisation against invasion had been directed towards Portugal, but as time went on it was assumed, because of the unexpectedly long delay in the departure of the English fleet, that the English were too weak or too ill-equipped to make the attempt, and this had led to the relaxation in preventative measures in both Spain and Portugal, to the point that orders were neglected to be carried out.

Thus Drake's sudden departure from England, with his joint-stock Armada of 125 ships and his arrival off Spain after only six days sailing before a favourable wind, surprised everyone, most of all the Spanish government, which, people believed, was always watchful and alert in anticipating events, however in this case it had been completely deceived by the speed and supposed cunning of the English. Incidentally, it is interesting to note that in Spanish accounts it is the name of the dreaded Drake that appears constantly. Even after the army landed Norris is rarely mentioned even though he was the soldier and Drake was the sailor.

From the Escorial, Philip, on receiving the news, immediately sent couriers to all the seaports, from Galicia in the north to Cadiz in the south, to warn them to be ready. Commanders were sent to their posts and preparations were ordered to be speeded up. All over the country people were blaming each other for the slowness of preparations when everyone had known for months that the English were putting together a fleet.

The commander-in-chief appointed to the forces of the Spanish counter-attack was Don Ernando de Toledo, son of the renowned hero of the Low Countries, the Duke of Alva. Don Ernando was a very experienced soldier, having served under his father. The navy on the other hand was not ready to challenge the English fleet. Despite English fears of another Armada, there was a shortage of ships and a shortage of workmen to build and repair those in the docks.

The general shortage of manpower meant that even Portuguese were enlisted, some of whom could be relied upon and some of whom, given the opportunity, it was feared, would use their weapons against their Spanish overlords. As an insurance policy, the leaders among the Portuguese nobility had been removed to Madrid and the Spanish felt sure that without them the ordinary people would be harmless.

Troops were to be collected from overseas, 6,000 from Italy, 2,000 from Tuscany, 3,000 from Calabria, and 1,000 from Lombardy. Italian galleys were to be brought into Spanish Mediterranean waters to safeguard against any activity on the part of the Turks or the Moroccans in support of Elizabeth. In addition to this, perhaps to reassure themselves, the Spanish believed that with the forces Drake was known to have at his disposal he could do no more than skirmish along the coasts and not be able to penetrate far inland.

But why, against Queen Elizabeth's strict and clear orders did the English Armada go to Coruna at all? It was at the port of Santander to the east that forty ships were being refitted in readiness for the next Armada, with another twenty in other ports, but not at Coruna, where there was only one vessel. It can only be that after months of being cooped up on short rations in constant readiness to set sail, the 23,000 men, mostly "the scum of the earth," were on the point of mutiny and so the promised inducement of loot, plunder and wealth had to be fulfilled. The Spanish, however, were ignorant of this and believed instead that it was part of some master plan. From their point of view, the attack was thought to be a tactical move, and gave it more credit than it warranted.

They believed that if the English possessed Coruna it would make a convenient base for further operations of harassment against Spain and Portugal. It would be a suitably convenient port to be reinforced and supplied from England. Another possible objective could be to rouse and give encouragement to the Portuguese, who had given signs of their intention to support the English and to revolt, and so divert any Spanish forces that might be sent to hold them in check.

The town of Coruna itself was weak and ill-garrisoned. It was the seat of the Viceroy and the Council of Galicia and its fall would mean the loss of the Marquis of Ceralba, the Governor. In the opinion of Don Ernando, the newly appointed commander of the Spanish forces, if the English took the town they could isolate it completely by cutting through the narrow neck of land that joined it to the mainland. After all, the English had brought 3,000 sappers with picks, shovels and everything else necessary for the work. Don Ernando was also keenly aware that Coruna had only one line of ancient defensive walls that were without flanking works or earth works; the fort of San Antonio was under-manned, and the town in fact would be in danger of falling to the enemy. He was to comment later, on 16th May, that he was surprised that it had not fallen sooner. On the other hand, he also believed that even if Drake were to take the town he could not keep it, for it was neither defensibly strong nor geographically safe, nor could Drake push far inland due to the limited numbers of his troops.

It was the Spanish belief that Drake had only 15,000 men available, 5,000 of whom, they surmised, would be needed to left to protect the ships, and so with 10,000 soldiers unsupported by cavalry he could not achieve much because there were already 10,000 Spanish troops in Portugal, and these would be supplemented by a further 10,000 when Don Ernando arrived accompanied by 1,000 cavalry, and then Drake would be driven out.

The Spanish people knew little about what was happening at Coruna. After the first reports no further news was heard in Madrid, even in the royal court there was no word from the city. There are two possible reasons for this, either the Marquis de Ceralba was completely blockaded and communications had been cut, or, King Philip had imposed strict censorship and forbade any announcements because he did not wish to alarm the people for reasons of morale. What is known is that at a pass called El Spinar, any letters arriving there were directed to the Escorial, a short distance away.

Coruna was indeed taken utterly by surprise. Drake was held in almost mythical awe by the Spanish, with his nickname of 'El Draco', the Dragon, he was the bogey man with whom Spanish parents would scare their children if they misbehaved. His sudden appearance with all his fleet terrified the totally unprepared inhabitants of the city and the countryside around. If anything, their expectation had been that the English fleet was destined for France and not for the Spanish coast, as the relaxation of preparations for defence and the neglect of orders clearly showed.

The people of Galicia had been going about their normal daily lives, the Cortes were in session at the time, the soldiers of the garrison happened to be nearly all on leave and so were scattered over the province. There was not time to evacuate the non-combatants or for them to hide their valuable possessions.

At the first alarm the wife and daughter of Marquis de Ceralba fled on foot in panic through the night six miles to a place of safety. They were among the very few who were able to do so, soon after that no one dared move from the city.

To defend the town there were only about 200 soldiers and the inhabitants, whose value was held to be of little account. In a hurried consultation the citizens prepared what defence they could. The lower part of the town fronting the harbour was protected on the land side only by weak walls, and was unfit for a protracted defence. The townspeople therefore had to acknowledge that if the place were attacked from the water side it would be untenable, and so it was arranged that as soon as those living on the hill in the higher part of the town should catch sight of the approaching English boats they were to signal the lower town by a fire, so that the people there might make their escape to the better defensible upper town.

The English fleet moved closer in, pushing their ships into the harbour. 8,000 men were disembarked to be landed on shore at a little bay within a mile of Coruna. There they were formed into various squadrons and posted around the town. No one opposed their landing and the soldiers were nearly at the town gates before a hasty muster of townsfolk met them. These civilians, unprepared and surprised as they were, soon retreated when they saw the force that was coming against them, and so shut themselves up behind the town's gates and walls.

But Coruna, commanded by the Marquis de Ceralba, being weakly defended and ill-garrisoned, could not hope to hold out against a regular siege. Ceralba hoped for help to arrive from troops commanded by Don Pedro de Sottomayor, but he was afraid that they would arrive too late. The town was not rated highly in military terms by the Spanish, there were three Spanish galleons in the harbour, laden with arms, munitions and other war supplies, which Don Ernando cynically said would be a much greater loss than the town itself. He left the Escorial for Zamora to the north-west on his way to Galicia and King Philip cancelled his journey to Valladolid, even though there was a greater need for it now than before, in order to be nearer the theatre of action. Meanwhile news came from the Cardinal Archduke Albert of Austria, who was governing

Portugal on Philip's behalf, that there was greater fear among the Spaniards of the Portuguese than of Drake's soldiers.

On their first night ashore the English army slept in the cottages and mills of a hamlet on the bank of one of the small rivers that flowed into the bay, which was out of gunshot of the town walls. They were quite unmolested by the terrified townsfolk, although from the harbour the Spanish galleon '*San Juan*' and her two consorts, together with the guns of the city, kept up a good fire on the soldiers as they passed to and fro. The galleys were frustrated in any action because they were unable to receive orders from the Marquis, their commander.

Next day, the 5th May, four pieces of English artillery were landed from the fleet and the guns bombarded the Spanish ships and galleys in order to stop their interfering fire. During the morning Coruna was attacked simultaneously from the bay by 1,200 men under Captain Fenner and Colonel Huntley, who approached in long boats and pinnaces, and by land from soldiers under Colonels Brett and Umpton on one side, and Captains Richard Wingfield and Sampson on the other side by escalade of the town walls.

The people in the upper town, either from panic or oversight, neglected to give the fire signal to the people of the lower town, who, as a result, believed that they had only to deal with the escalade led by Captain Wingfield, and fought desperately until they found two other forces had entered the town at three other points. At this, panic seized them, and as an English observer wrote, "with an huge crie, the inhabitants betooke them to the high towne, which they might with less peril doo for that our being strangers knew not the way to cut them off. The rest that were not put to the sword in furie fled to the rockes on the island and hid themselves in chambers and sellers which were every day found out in great numbers." The people did right to panic; the suburbs were sacked and, "the butchery that followed was inhuman."

Following this, in the evening the English made a landing in many boats to attack the fish market, the Pexaderia, and successfully seized and occupied it. The Venetian ambassador, in one of his reports from Madrid to the Doge in Venice, was later to comment that Drake, by knocking down houses, seizing cattle, killing soldiers, releasing officers on ransom, and by pillaging the suburbs, the surrounding villages and the burning of the monasteries, seemed to care more for plunder than for glory. In fact Drake and Norris were now able to add to their supplies 6,000 salted oxen, 15,000 'cantaras' (pitchers containing about four or five gallons) of biscuits, 6,000 barrels of powder, and 3,000 hogsheads of wine, all of which had been destined either to supply King Philip's Armada of the previous year or else the one he was proposing for the following year. This increase in sustenance took the pressure off the expedition's commanders, who had been awaiting supplies from England. The loss also caused great mortification within the Spanish government, where news from Coruna was kept secret, censored or minimised as much as possible.

Early the next day the lower part of the city of Coruna was completely invested, entrenchments were dug and Norris's troops were reported to the Spanish to be well-disciplined. At 11 o'clock a bombardment of the high town commenced. By 1 o'clock, after an attack of two hours continuous fire, although from only a few guns, the old lower town walls, which were very weak, were levelled to the ground and one of the towers was wrecked. The command for the assault was then given but after two hours fighting without success, the English withdrew. Drake and Norris were later to complain that the artillery they had at their disposal was insufficient to undertake a full-scale siege.

This withdrawal was not so much a lack of success, but more that the attack had been a complete failure. The English army, according to the Spanish, had even kept their Royal Standard down on the ground for a considerable time during the day. A large number of English officers were lost, and in their retreat the army left a great quantity of arms. The Spanish reported a loss of about twelve of their best men, and that in all the skirmishes, losses finally totalled about 100 killed and 150 wounded, whereas, they claimed, the English lost 1,500 men, including an officer of the Queen, who was her prime favourite, who, although he was not named, they knew had an income of 12,000 ducats, and who had borne the Royal Standard.

In the meantime all Galicia was arming. A Spanish prisoner who had been brought in by English cattle raiders gave away the information that the Count de Andrada was six miles away at Puente de Burgos with 8,000 men, and this was believed to be only the beginning of a great army being got together by the Count de Altamira. The Spanish believed that Drake would withdraw after a few days, if the city could hold out long enough to receive the support that was on its way.

Not one to waste time, that same day, 6th May, Sir Edward Norris determined to attack the Spanish, so with nine regiments he marched out to meet Count de Andrada. The vanguard of the English army was divided into three bodies, commanded by Captains Middleton, Ethrington, and Anthony Wingfield, who attacked the Spaniards simultaneously in the centre and on both flanks, routing them at the first charge. The Spanish only stopped in their retreat when they came to a fortified bridge over a creek of the sea, on the other side of which was their entrenched camp. Norris, together with Colonel Sidney and Captains Fulford and Hinder and others who, according to an English propagandist, were always at the front, fought hand to hand over the bridge and into the Spanish trenches, under "an incredible volie of shot for that the shot of their armies flanked upon both sides of the bridge."

Norris, in his eagerness to be first, tumbled over his pike and badly injured his head. Nearly all the officers of the vanguard were more or less hurt, but their injuries were rewarded when the defensive earthworks were soon abandoned. After the Spanish soldiers fled, the usual "amusement of the common sort" commenced for the English army. The countryside for miles around was burnt and wasted, and the fleeing people were slaughtered without mercy or quarter. "So many as 2,000 men might kill in pursuit, so many fell before us that day," a diarist recorded.

When the rampage was over, while the men were returning to Corunna, hundreds of peasants were found scattered, hidden cowering in hedges and vineyards, and the soldiers cut their throats. Two hundred peasants took refuge in a church which the English burned down, and any men who tried to escape were put to the sword. "You might have seen the countrie more than three miles of compasse on fyre," wrote the diarist.

From experience Drake knew that idleness and boredom in the ranks led to discontent and trouble, so he had diverted the men's attention by allowing them this action. But, as looters, the improvised army saw only what was in front of them and gave no thought to what was to happen next. Material gain was what they had come for, and it was the sole motive for the soldiers and ships crews. An absolute orgy was indulged in by the troops, for here was the realisation of their dreams and aspirations, and a fulfilment of the promises made at their recruitment – there was a fleeing, panic-stricken enemy, ample plunder to loot and to waste, and, above all, wine without limit. Some Spaniards surrendered to be taken alive as prisoners and ransomed if possible, but the rest, numbering up to about 500 who fell into the hands of the common soldiers, had had their throats cut.

With possible exaggeration it was said that every cellar was found to be full of wine, and through excessive drinking the men became senseless and careless of the danger of gunfire from the town by which many of them were killed and wounded. Later on it was believed that it was through the drink that men first became ill with the sickness that was to take a great toll in fatalities and generally severely reduced the effectiveness of the army.

Sickness was a fact of life on board ship in the 16th century, due mainly to the careless practices of sailors. Seamen were disorderly by nature and lived a hard life on board, where disease was common in the confined, overcrowded, unventilated, unhealthy living quarters that, together with vermin, provided a breeding ground for contagion. The disease that was to ravage the fleet and the army was probably scurvy, caused by a generally poor diet, a lack of fresh food, and impure drinking water.

The Spanish government was to excuse itself for the easy defeat of Count de Andrada's army by saying that the wars in the Netherlands and the fears for Portugal and the French frontier had denuded all north-western Spain of good soldiers, and that the force of Andrada was only a hastily assembled levy of undrilled and practically unarmed countrymen, who were easily routed.

The Spanish, although well-informed in many respects, were still uncertain as to Drake's intentions. They were very much afraid that if Don Antonio was with the fleet, as they believed he was, then Drake would sail along the coast of Portugal and try to cause a sudden uprising for which, at the time, the Portuguese were quite ripe.

At Coruna in addition to the great quantities of provisions found in the lower town, many more supplies were captured for the benefit of the expedition when they were brought in by unsuspecting Spanish ships. The provisions were alleged by the Drake and Norris to have been collected by the Spanish for the purpose of supplying a new attack on England, which was quite probably the case, although conclusive proof was lacking. At all events, the prevention of these supplies being delivered to the Spanish was in the end the only act which justified in any sense the expedition sent out by the adventurers.

The next few days at Coruna were spent in desultory attacks by the invaders on the upper town. The monastery of St. Dominic was burnt, and the country around was scoured by Colonel Huntly, who brought in a large number of cows and sheep that helped to feed the 23,000 men.

After days of unproductive pottering about, the troops were presumably sober enough to attempt an attack upon the upper town, where the fortress had no support except from the peasantry. With the English cannon pointing at it, the position of the fort was hopeless, so Norris sent a drummer to demand that it surrender before he opened fire. However, the summons was answered by a musket-shot that killed the drummer. Immediately afterwards a pole was projected over the town wall from which a body was dangling by the neck.

This was the man who had fired the cowardly shot. Then the Spaniards called for a parley and begged that the battle might be honourable on both sides, as it certainly would be on theirs. Considering that 500 of their people had had their throats savagely cut after they had surrendered, this was magnanimous to say the least, but the defenders would not be persuaded to surrender the town.

For three more days Norris continued to blast away with his cannon at the high town in an attempt to make a breach in the wall, while at the same time he set the sappers to work to bore a mine through the rock towards the gate. When everything was ready and his troops, under the command of the Wingfield brothers and Captains Philpot, Sampson and York, were waiting to storm the two breaches, the mine turned out to be a dismal failure and so nothing was done.

'Black Jack' Norris was dreaded almost as much as Drake himself, and his skill and daring suggested to the terrified Spanish court that he might intend to cut through the neck of land upon which Coruna stood, to isolate the town entirely, which he then might make into a great depot for an English fleet.

The position for the defenders was becoming desperate. The fort, which had been weak to begin with, had been heavily bombarded, the garrison, which was below strength in any case, had been further reduced, and now their powder was running short. Supplies by sea had been repulsed and the ships bringing them were forced to retire. The Marquis of Ceralba, who was defending the fort, was still hoping for help from Don Pedro de Sottomayor, but he was afraid that it would arrive after the need for it had passed, so the besiegers did what they could and strengthened their position by strategically placing their artillery.

One report the Marquis wrote read, "I will only say that we have not more than 300 men of the Seville reserves who will fight, and some few of the district; we are without provisions which were all burned in the firing of the fish market; and very little ammunition. On the night of the capture of the fish-market Don Juan de Lusia and Don Juan de Monsalutio and other officers were made prisoners."

Some young hotheads of the nobility of the Spanish court had set off for Coruna without authority or arms and in no order, but they were ordered to return by the king, who thought they might do more harm than good. Philip in the meanwhile was accumulating both money and an army, and there was confidence that the English would be driven off, but the opinion was that it would have been better to have done this beforehand for prevention rather than as a cure after the arrival of the enemy.

It was felt that King Philip was insulted, not so much by the actual events at Coruna, but by his opponents, Queen Elizabeth, Sir Francis Drake and Sir John Norris, "the fact that a woman, mistress of only half an island, with the help of a corsair and a common soldier, should have ventured on so arduous an enterprise, and dared to molest so powerful a sovereign."

Beyond that, there was concern that if Coruna fell, the English would attack Santander next, where many ships did actually lie at anchor, and this, after all, was one of the named targets of the expedition. In the port of Santander there were forty ships that, with a further twenty elsewhere, made a total of sixty towards the intended new Armada, therefore the fort at Santander, with its natural defences, had been re-garrisoned.

Couriers were sent to all the seaports on the coast from Galicia to Cadiz to warn them to be ready against the foe. Officers were dispatched to take command, and all other preparations were hurried on. The Spanish navy was nowhere near ready to take on the English fleet, work on the new ships was even then proceeding very slowly due to the lack of workmen. As well as this, the navy was not complete due to a lack of competent officers. On the other hand there was confidence that, due to the strength of the garrisons of the coastal forts, Drake would only be able to plunder open ports and bombard unfortified towns rather than undertake an invasion.

But leaving nothing to chance, the people in Portugal had been armed, although there was doubt as to their reliability, so as a safeguard, potential leaders and supporters of Don Antonio with his English allies had been arrested. Luckily at sea the galleys had arrived from Italy to prevent the threat from the shereef of Morocco and the Turks, who were receiving encouragement from Queen Elizabeth.

The next day the 9th of May the English sappers tried again to undermine the walls of Coruna, and this time they did it with such success that one half of the gate tower was blown up and the other half was left teetering. The assailants then rushed in, a few of whom actually got into the town, but just as the officers and the men immediately following set foot on the breach in the wall to wave their men on, the other half of the tower came crashing down, crushing them under the rubble. In the melee two English standards were lost and recaptured, and scores of men were killed. In the dust and terror the inexperienced English soldiers thought they were the victims of a clever enemy strategem and turned and ran, leaving the officers and gentlemen volunteers to extricate themselves as best they could. A Captain Sydenham "was pitifully lost, who having three or four great stones on his lower parts was held so fast, as neither himself could stirre, nor anie reasonable companie recover him. Notwithstanding the next day being found to be alive there was ten or twelve (men) lost in attempting to relieve him."

It was at this point that a local heroine became a Spanish legend. As the attackers forced the breach in the walls of the old upper city, and Spanish troops and citizens were doing all they could to hold out against them, an army captain was killed by a shot from a crossbow bolt to the head. A woman fighting nearby was his wife, who killed an English soldier as he struggled up the rubble in an attempt to plant a banner on a high point on the wall. The woman was Maria Pita. Legend has it that she appeared in the thick of the fray shouting "Whoever has honour, follow me!" She now has a statue to her in a square named after her in Coruna, and there is the Maria Pita House museum in the city. She went on to live a long life from 1565 to 1643, married four times and had four children. Other women of the city of course also took part in its defence, one of whom was Ines de Ben, who was wounded twice by musket shots and was later honoured by King Philip, who granted her the pension of a military officer, which she received after the death of her husband who was also killed during the siege.

Maria Pita, heroine of Coruna

On the other side of the town a breach made by the culverin cannon in the town walls was too small for a general assault, and when Captain York led his men to a 'push-of-pike' (one step removed from hand-to-hand combat) with the defenders who stood in the breach, the steep slope of the heap of rubble up which they were climbing suddenly slipped to leave the attackers six feet lower than the opening, and so they had to retreat. The only way back for them was through a narrow lane where the soldiers had to run the gauntlet, being exposed to the full fire of the defenders. So the attack on the upper town had failed at both points. But by now the already weak defences of the fort had been bombarded to the point that they were hardly defensible, the garrison was running short of powder, the reliefs sent to their aid had been repulsed and the English had been able to consolidate the positions of their artillery to repel any relief column. Anxiety was growing in Spain about what Drake and the English might do if they held on to Coruna.

Drake and Norris sent favourable accounts of their success home with Sir William Knollys, who listed the companies and order of assault against the 'Lower Town of the Groyne,' the names of the colonels and companies engaged with the enemy, and the order of battle in which they were placed. The two commanders also asked for more provisions from England and for more money. When Knollys gave his report of the success at Coruna to Elizabeth, she was not fooled, she was in "a towering rage," she was not to be appeased, she said that they ought to have gone and burnt the ships at Santander before going to the Groyne, she knew they had gone more for profit than for service, and she could still neither forget nor forgive the absence of Essex, her favourite. Although Essex was a very minor side issue to the expedition as a whole, the queen was the queen and Walter Raleigh and Charles Blount were all very well in their way, but she wanted Essex, and she suspected Drake and Norris of being complicit in his escape.

It was remarked that "She is strangely informed against them." On the 14th May she wrote a remarkable letter to her Drake and Norris, upbraiding them for perverting the prime objectives of the enterprise, which were to destroy the king of Spain's navy, to restore Don Antonio to the throne of Portugal, and then to proceed to the Azores. She noted that they had neglected two places where they ought to have gone and burnt ships before going to Coruna. Coruna, she said, was of little importance and the risk to the expedition was great, she commanded them to fulfil her orders at once. Also they were not to harbour illusions of glory for themselves that would obscure their judgement.

Showing that she knew of Essex being on board the *Swiftsure*, she demanded dire vengeance on Sir Roger Williams, whom she knew had hidden him and had had the temerity to abscond with one of her own ships. She said of Drake and Norris, "If they have not already inflicted punishment of death upon him (Williams) he is to be deprived of all command and kept in safe custody at their perils. If the Earl of Essex has joined the fleet they are to send him home instantly. If they do not they shall truly answer for the same at their smart, for as we have authority to rule so do we look to be obeyed and these by no childish actions." She claimed that she was surprised by their demands for men and munitions after her £20,000, but nevertheless, the re-supply ships had been inspected and would be ready to sail by the 22nd of the month.

The draft of this letter, which was deeply scored by the Elizabeth's own hand, was submitted to Walsingham by Windebanke, the Secretary of the Signet, and the minister commented that, although the letter was as mild as could be expected "under the circumstances," he very much feared that any measures taken against one so popular as Sir Roger Williams would lead to mutiny. Apparently generals Drake and Norris agreed with this for they dared boldly to take no notice of the Elizabeth's dire commands.

Meanwhile during the siege other things were happening. One day a great crowd of country people armed with crude weapons came down "at a run" to see what manner of men they were who raided their cattle and burnt their homes, but a volley of musketry from the English killed eighteen of them and sent the rest running away. It was reported in Madrid that although the mass of people was supposed to have numbered about 2,400, they had only six arquebusses between them. On another occasion, an improvised gabion protecting an English gun battery was shaken to pieces by the concussion from its first cannon shot, from which the town's defenders took full advantage, killing the lieutenant of the ordnance, Master Spenser, and many others as they stood in full view.

However Sir Edward Norris held his ground until orders came for him to cease firing and retire. A Captain Goodwin, after he had misunderstood a signal, prematurely attacked the upper town only to be shot through the mouth, while many of the "common sort" of soldiery who fell out through drink, pestilence and wounds, went unrecorded by name.

During their preparation for departure from Curuna, the English burnt the fish market and all the houses and mills around the town, in addition to the monastery. They burnt five Spanish ships in the harbour, including the galleons, *San Mino* and *San Juan*, the Duke's admiral's ship. In the harbour only the *San Bernado* remained intact; she cut her cables and drifted onto the shore under the town; of the others, some had been burned by order of the Marquis and the remainder by the English. As this news arrived in England, it was faithfully relayed back to Spain by 'David' the spy.

The next day, the 19th, after again unsuccessfully trying to set fire to the upper town, the English began to ship their artillery and baggage and began to get ready to depart. To King Philip, despite the failure of the English assault, the bitterest blow was the knowledge that Spain's impotence was now obvious to the world, and that the mere presence of Drake was sufficient to paralyse all resistance. Philip was told that the people of Coruna were so glad to be rid of him at any cost, that when the English force re-embarked it was not even molested.

In the meantime utter dismay reigned at Madrid. What was left of the Armada fleet was acknowledged to be powerless even for defence, and no one knew for certain where the next English blow would fall. The reports from Coruna had been intercepted by the Government and were surmised to be worse than they really were; but still general opinion was not far out in supposing that Drake and his forces could not do much permanent harm to the open places on the coast, and that they would eventually attack either Lisbon or Cadiz.

The Spanish court believed, falsely, that while Drake was at Coruna he was so strongly entrenched that he suffered no loss at all. Even so, Philip was aware of the irony that if the English had remained only a few days longer the town would have fallen, because the expected relief was not so ready as had been rumoured.

Don Fernando de Toldedo was appointed commander-in-chief of the army, but the soldiers could not be got together. This led to a bitter joke in Madrid that whereas the Armada the year before had an army with no commander, there was now a commander with no army. Due to the shortage of soldiers a measure had been taken that was considered to be possibly more harmful than helpful, which was that the hitherto unreliable Portuguese had been enlisted, that although the Spanish had "armed the very people they have cause to fear, but perhaps they think that as they have destroyed the leaders they have made themselves safe."

Back in England there were the re-supply ships which had been inspected and would be ready to sail on the 22nd of the month. There was a rumour, a false one as it turned out in the end, that Al-Mansur had supplied gunpowder to the English. Letters went between courtiers saying that the queen was by now thoroughly disenchanted with the expedition, and that she was "intensely incensed" at the fruitless attack on Coruna.

The English fleet lay all night about five miles offshore from Coruna, being unable to sail around Cape Finisterre due to contrary winds. The Duke of Alva and the Duke of Francavilla finally arrived at the city with their men, which meant that the aid from distant Castile had come in before that from Galicia, but too late all the same.

Tension and dismay were keenly felt in Spain, a commentator wrote, "Their (The English fleet) route is for some point between the (River) Douro and the (River) Mino; and we are not yet free of anxiety, for we left in the morning for Bayona to support it in case of need, with the miserable troops which the people of this country have shown themselves to be, and the saying is true that the great is the shame and the poverty of those who have to live among them. God grant us better fortune than in the past, for it is a sheer miracle that this city was not lost, in defence of which I will not recount the actions of the Marquis."

Peniche

Late in the day of 19th of May, the entire English force was back on board ship and the fleet departed from Coruna on the 20th, leaving behind them smoking ruins for many miles around. The Spanish chose to believe that Drake's decision to leave was prompted by reports that twelve of their galleys were on their way from Lisbon to relieve Coruna, collecting more troops en route.

The fleet had sailed with a fair wind, but the 'fair wind' did not last long, and contrary winds drove the ships back time and again, so they had to keep to the open sea. In fact Drake was driven back along the coasts that he had already raided, so there was nothing left to plunder, and, what was more, the Spanish coast was now garrisoned.

A happy event occurred on the 21st when the Dutch flyboats arrived with reinforcements of 200 men, having been separated from the main fleet off the coast of Spain. Then, at last on the 23rd of May, the truant ship *Swiftsure* hove into sight, "to the great delight of us all," said one eye-witness, bringing the Earl of Essex, Sir Roger Williams, Master Walter Devereux, the earl's brother, who was "a gentleman of wonderful great hope", Sir Philip Butler, "who hath always been most inward with him", and Sir Edward Wingfield.

The Earl of Essex, having joined the expedition against everyone's advice and at the risk of his own fortune, intended to enhance his reputation but, although he was highly thought of, his rash behaviour was often wondered at. He had deliberately avoided the Queen's messengers who were sent after him demanding his return, and he was supposed to have other reasons to avoid them that were known only to himself. As if to justify himself and prove his bravery, the earl's first request was that he should always be allowed to lead the vanguard of the army, a request that was easily granted, because everyone was anxious to please him. So, after this and until the end of the expedition he marched at the head of the column with the other 'prodigal,' Major-General Sir Roger Williams, who himself seemed "not one penny the worse" for Elizabeth's antipathy.

However glad the men of lower rank may have been to see that dashing young nobleman, Essex, Drake and Norris could hardly have been overjoyed. They knew by this time that Elizabeth was in earnest; that the purse-strings would be drawn tighter, and, so long as her errant favourite was with the expedition, her censure would be stricter.

On 24th May part of the expedition, consisting of seventy English ships, was sighted off the coast of Portugal. The Spanish were still trying to guess the English intentions; from their point of view one possibility was that the fleet could ravage the coast of Portugal while at the same time keeping the Spanish fleet divided. This could be easily made possible due to the general speed in action of the English and the general slowness of the Spanish. They also worried that the fleet would sail to take the islands of Azores which were so important for navigation to the West Indies, and were weakly garrisoned by only about 1,000 men, who were hated by the locals, or else to seize some of the fifty or sixty richly-laden ships that were in the vicinity, against which the Spanish were powerless to act, having no ships ready to defend them.

However, after several days at sea, when Drake and Norris were optimistically expecting another fifty ships with reinforcements and provisions to appear at any time, early in the afternoon of May 26th the English fleet, with 154 sail, fifty other boats and upwards of 20,000 men divided between the sailors and troops on board, cautiously approached the Portuguese town of Peniche, which was "a small place and no harbour," but only about forty miles from Lisbon.

One of the reasons for landing at Peniche was that Drake, on his way south, had heard that a great galleon from the East Indies with a million crowns in gold had taken refuge in Peniche under the guns of the fortress and, being Drake, he hoped to capture this huge prize. However he was thwarted in his aim because Cardinal Archduke Albert in Lisbon had also been anxiously looking out for the gold, and he had sent galleys under the command of Bazan to bring the galleon into the River Tagus, which they did just three days before the English arrived at Peniche.

The Spanish were slightly mystified by the landing because the town of Peniche was of no size or strategic importance, nor was it well fortified. Nevertheless, Don Pedro de Guzman, the Inspector General, was sent from Lisbon with three companies, amounting to 300 to 350 Spanish infantry and 3,000 Portuguese infantry, to oppose the landing. Juan Gonzalez de Ataide held the town of Peniche with a body of Portuguese, who could not be trusted, in the small inadequately fortified with its garrison of 1,000 foot and 200 horse, part of which was the normal garrison and the rest had been sent from Lisbon. A drawn-out siege was at first anticipated.

On sighting the English fleet De Ateide drew up his men at the landing place in front of the fortress and as the enemy ships entered the bay he opened fire on them, although at the time the Spanish were not clear what the English objective was. A mile and a half away on the beach of Consolation, over on the other side of the harbour where the surf was running high, and where a landing there was thought to be impracticable, the shore had been left undefended. Suddenly, when the Spaniards least expected it, Sir Edward Norris began to land his men there. The hot-headed Essex did not even wait for his boat to reach land, he jumped into the beating surf breast high with Sir Roger Williams and a band of gentlemen and struggled ashore to protect the landing of the rest.

De Ateide and his troops raced around the bay but by the time they reached the place 4,000 English with fifty horse and some supply wagons had been landed. They were at first repulsed by the son of the Duke of Villareale with losses on both sides. The Spanish made a brave show of resistance but they were heavily out-numbered, and after fifteen of them had fallen at the push-of-pike they were nearly surrounded so they were forced to retire inland to a neighbouring hamlet where De Ateide waited for reinforcements from the town of Torres Vedras to the south.

Although several boatloads were lost in the surf, within four hours Norris had landed the balance of 12,000 or 13,000 men including, so the Spanish believed, up to 600 Spaniards. Without further molestation from the Spanish, Norris summoned Captain Araujo, the Portuguese commander of the fortress, to surrender. The English expected a siege and if that happened the outcome would be in doubt because, being so close to Lisbon, the capital, it could be readily reinforced from other places. Captain Araujo replied firmly to Norris that he refused to surrender to the English, however he would willingly do so to Don Antonio, his lawful king who had also landed.

On his arrival in Peniche De Guzman could do nothing because all the inhabitants had fled. He had attempted to prevent the landing of the English troops, but all the Portuguese soldiers took flight when the fleet anchored, although their officers did their duty well. De Guzman received support in the form of 200 additional fresh troops, but even with their help, after he had skirmished at one end of the landing place, he was forced to retire because Captain Araujo, the commander of the fortress who was known to be secretly in favour of Don Antonio, had abandoned the place when his garrison fled, and he himself set off for Lisbon.

During the night after the landing some cavalry under Captain Alarcon had joined the waiting Spaniards. A force of Portuguese militia had also been sent in by Don Luis Alencastro, the Grand-Commander of the Order of Christ, but these men soon deserted and left the officers to shift for themselves. The next morning at four o'clock Alarcon and a few of the Spanish cavalry went to reconnoitre the position at Peniche, but found the English to be too many for them, so they could only ride back as hard as they could to Alencastro, a few miles away on the road to Lisbon, who was endeavouring to reorganise a body of Portuguese. Terrible tales of the strength of the English had already been spread about, so when Alarcon and De Guzman reached Alencastro they found his hastily-raised levies in a state of panic at a rumour that Drake had brought with him 900 great Irish dogs as fierce as lions, and "capable of eating up a world of folks," and were flatly refusing to move. Alencastro therefore could do nothing more than hurry back to Lisbon to inform Cardinal-Archduke Albert of the state of affairs, while De Guzman, with the troops, fell back upon the town of Torres-Vedras, if possible to hold the road to Lisbon.

News of these events was kept from the Spanish people in Madrid. There was particular fear that the presence of Don Antonio would cause an uprising in Portugal, where the people were restive. After the discovery of several conspiracies aimed at helping Don Antonio onto the throne, some of the plotters were executed and others imprisoned. These plots had been revealed by one of the Portuguese spies who had been with Don Antonio in England but was loyal to Spain. The man was probably Diego Rodriguez who had been treasurer to the expedition.

This supposed friend had made his escape at Coruna and gone straight to Philip at the Escorial to divulge all Don Antonio's plans, including a copy of the agreement between Don Antonio and Queen Elizabeth in which the "pretender" promised much more than repayment, together with the names of his supporters who were still in Portugal and ready to help him into Lisbon. These people were all arrested, so that by the time Don Antonio arrived at Peniche the Spanish said he found no one but monks and commoners to greet him.

Philip was still planning to go to Valladolid against the wishes of his advisors. The archers of the bodyguard had been paid and the final call for horse to be ready on the 15th June had been made. This activity on behalf of the king failed to influence the defence of Galicia and Portugal where the military preparations continued to proceed at a slow pace.

When, after years in exile, Don Antonio at last landed on Portuguese soil with his son Manuel, and his bodyguard of a hundred Portuguese, to be received once more in his own land as a sovereign, he found that everything had been prepared for him. His canopy of state was erected, the plate for his table was set out and his subjects knelt before him "seeking for his smiles." His bodyguard was supplied with muskets and pikes from the castle and he kept court in the town for two days.

He was recorded as speaking fairly and smoothly to the country people, from whom he took nothing, but gave them, or at least promised them, much, and he assured them all of his royal protection. But if King Antonio did not wish to oppress the people, the Spanish overlords had no such scruples. The soldiers retaliated against Araujo's treachery in surrendering Peniche by stealing everything they could lay their hands on that belonged to the Portuguese. In one case, possibly using the confusion as a cover, they took the large sum of two thousand crowns from one of the most influential Portuguese friends of the Spanish cause.

As the supposedly rightful King of Portugal Don Antonio was conscious of his regal dignity and he had many little wrangles with the English about the scant ceremony with which they treated him. One can imagine that for them his royal cause to regain the throne was only incidental to their quest for plunder.

King Philip had been too cunning for his enemy. He had banished every Portuguese noble—seventy of them in all—who was not tied hard and fast to the Spanish cause to distant places in Spain at the moment when Don Antonio depended on the country to flock to his call for the independence of Portugal with himself as king. The lower religious orders, the friars, and peasants did come in to salute their native king, but the lords and gentry from whom he expected so much did not appear. The remaining gentry that he did see were usually too panic-stricken to side with him, openly or otherwise, having seen the fate of the others.

Despite Spanish anxiety about the arrival of Don Antonio with his heretic English allies, there was a prevailing doubt that even if they did capture Lisbon that they could hold it against the might of Spain. It could only be done with the help of the ordinary citizens and there was doubt whether the Portuguese people would or could rise without their nobles to lead them. In addition there was an underlying concern among the people about the treatment they would receive from the heretic English if they once got the upper hand without the nobles to restrain them.

However, Don Antonio was confident that the country would rise up in his support, and he was now eager to push on to his capital of Lisbon, which, he was sure, was waiting for him with open arms. His confidence seems to a certain extent to have been shared by Norris, and it was here that the second great mistake of the expedition was made. The first vital error had been the fruitless waste of time at Corunna; the second was the resolution now arrived at by Don Antonio and Norris, which was entirely against Drake's judgement, which was to march forty miles overland from Peniche to Lisbon. This decision may also have been influenced by the increasing tension between the two commanders.

Drake, with his maritime experience, was true to the sea and to the tactics that he had often used to beat the Spaniards, was in favour of pushing on to Lisbon by sea, so reaching the city much sooner. Once there, he proposed, he would let three or four fireships drift about the castle of San Gian, which commanded the entrance to the harbour, so that the smoke would spoil the aim of its guns, and then make a dash for the city – and doubtless, knowing Drake, also for the galleon with its million gold crowns that lay at anchor in front of the 'India' house. Don Antonio, whose one idea was to keep his feet on the land where he was king, sided with Norris. He believed that now he was King of Portugal on Portuguese soil he should be in overall command of the expedition.

But the fact was that he had for too long been a suppliant and a fugitive, dependent largely upon Elizabeth's whims and fancies for the English generals to take him seriously or regard him as anything but a tool for their own ends. A letter written around this time illustrated the not altogether happy relations that existed between the English forces and Don Antonio's Portuguese friends and bodyguard. Then there was tension now between the land commander Norris and the sea commander Drake. In vain Drake pointed out that the army had no baggage train or proper provisions for a long march through potentially hostile country, if the populace did not rally to aid the cause; that they had only one weak squadron of cavalry, which was out of condition by being on board ship for so long; the sickness that was beginning to show itself among the men; that they had no suitable field artillery; and that, once inland, they would lose the support and protection of the fleet.

His logic was to no avail, Don Antonio and Norris had their way. A single company was to be left to garrison Peniche, supported by six ships, and, while the whole of the land forces were to march to Lisbon, Drake was to take the rest of the fleet to the town of Cascais at the mouth of the River Tagus as soon as the weather would allow him to do so.

Spanish propaganda about Peniche later claimed that Drake had sacked and burned the town and that the Spanish troops "had made great havoc of the English."

Don Antonio and his army set out for Lisbon in anticipation that the people of Portugal would rise to support him. However, as well as having been influenced by Spanish stories, rumours and propaganda, the Portuguese people suspected and hated the heretic Protestant English allies more than they hated their Spanish oppressors. So, for one reason or another, hardly anyone on the road declared for Don Antonio. Archduke Albert, the governor in Lisbon, had had made sure of that. But in any case the country was poor and thinly populated, so no practical support for Don Antonio could have realistically been given, even if there had been the will.

The March

The English army, by all accounts 12,000 strong, after they had taken Peniche and the nearby village of Atouguia de Baleia, left 250 men in Peniche and marched out of the town on the 17th of May, with the Earl of Essex and Sir Roger Williams in the van. Drake accompanied them to the top of a hill at some distance off and greeted each regiment as it passed him with "kindly words, and hopes of success," success which he could scarcely hope for.

Soon the English soldiery began to show their true character. A strict order had been given that the property and persons of Don Antonio's faithful subjects were to be respected, but as soon as the army was clear of Peniche, housebreaking and pillage became rife, and Norris had to order his provost-marshal, Crisp, to hang a few of the malefactors before he could secure obedience.

To their credit, the soldiers obeyed the two rules imposed by the commanders, one to refrain from taking booty, the other to ostentatiously display images of the saints and to practise the Catholic religion, a situation that the Protestant English soldiers resented. It was a curious situation that Catholic King Don Antonio was to be put on the Portuguese throne by the heretic Protestant English queen.

However by not taking booty or plundering the countryside as they went, the army was not carrying out the usual practice of living off the land, so, as a consequence, as well as not taking provisions in the first place it caused them to run short of commons.

At first, word went among the English soldiers that a stand would be made by the Spaniards at a village not far from Peniche, but as they arrived the last Spanish horsemen were just leaving it. From Lisbon the Cardinal-Archduke had sent three squadrons of horsemen to reinforce Pedro de Guzman at the village of Torres Vedras, half way to Lisbon, in order to block the road and harass the English. Scouts went out to reconnoitre the English progress at various points after they left Peniche, but made no attempt to engage with them and each time fell back again to the village of Torres Vedras. Messengers were sent hourly to the Archduke begging for more men, whom he could not send.

The next day, the 18th, it was said with certainty that a great stand would be made at Torres Vedras, and this was undoubtedly the Archduke's intention, but even that almost impregnable village was untenable with only a few hundred horse, and a body of militia, who, if they fought at all, it was believed, would fight on the other side. So the Spanish forces, in fear of being cut off from their base, hastily evacuated Torres Vedras and gradually fell back, harassing the flanks of the English enemy as much as they could and cutting off stragglers.

Ignoring these "insect bites," the main body of Norris' force, with the Earl of Essex and Sir Roger Williams always in the lead, moved rapidly and untroubled towards Lisbon, while the panic in the capital became greater as the English drew near. The army was peaceable but hungry, for the land was bare, and what food the English did find was not to their taste, the local fare being, "dry and tasteless and [they] hankered after their own fat meats and birds, comparing our barrenness with the abundance of their own land." There was little or no money in the commissary, yet nothing was to be taken from the Portuguese without payment. There was in any case very little to take, for most of the people along the road had fled or had been stripped clean by the Spanish soldiers who had gone before in their retreat to the capital. Drake's predictions of trouble in moving an army without a baggage train began to come true, and at last starvation was breeding open mutiny in the English host.

Norris was obliged to tell Don Antonio that unless food was forthcoming more plentifully the soldiers must be allowed to shift for themselves. On Antonio's only response was to ask his controller, Campello, to scour the country far and wide for 'delicacies' for the English, "who are naturally dainty and exquisite in their food," for which he could only pay in promises, so the hungry invaders marched on towards Lisbon. From day to day Don Antonio and Norris were told that the Spaniards would certainly stand and fight tomorrow, but they were continually being disappointed, as indeed was the Archduke in his palace in Lisbon, who received with dismay the constant news that his forces were falling further and further back towards the capital without fighting.

Sir John Norris, commander of the English land forces

Whatever country people had remained on the road welcomed the army with cries of "Long Live King Don Antonio!" but their king looked in vain for the promised nobles and gentlemen. His desire to please his rustic adherents was described as almost pathetic. He condescended, it was haughtily observed, to "caress and embrace" the "commonest little people," but then he wanted to be 'beloved' of all of his subjects. In order to impress the English, he was supposed by his critics to have picked out any countryman who was decently spoken as some grand gentleman in disguise. But however hopeful he might show himself, he could not conceal the fact that not a dozen men-at-arms had joined him, and his only chance now was that Lisbon itself should declare in his favour.

On the 19th of May Norris and his troops marched into Torres Vedras, where Don Antonio was received with regal honours, the inhabitants came out with a canopy to welcome him, and the oath of allegiance to him was taken. Being very sure of himself, he wished to a lengthy detour to Santarem, some thirty-five miles to the east, through a rich country that was favourable towards him, but Norris knew the danger of delay and insisted on pushing forward to Lisbon.

De Guzman and his horsemen had fallen back during the previous night to Jara, nearer Lisbon, but he had left Captain Alarcon with two companies of horse to hang on the skirts of the enemy, skirmishing all the while. De Guzman and Alarcon later claimed to have killed many English while on their march. The next day Captain Yorke, commander of Norris's cavalry, decided to put the Spanish to the test. He sent a corporal with eight men who, so the English claimed, rode through forty of the Spanish, while Yorke himself with forty horse, put to flight Alarcon's two hundred. On the following day, May 21st, the English, without the satisfaction of a fight, were lodged in the village of Loures, about seven miles north of Lisbon, which Guzman had hurriedly evacuated after being very nearly surprised by Norris.

The village was small and the available accommodation was poor, so Drake's regiment, hoping to find better quarters, went to sleep at a little hamlet a mile off. In the early dawn a cry was raised of "Long Live King Don Antonio!" which was the usual friendly salutation of the country folk. The English sentries mingled with the people who approached and allowed them into their camp. But it was a trick, an ambush planned by the Spaniards, and many of the English were killed before the Spanish were finally driven off by two companies of English who were quartered nearby.

The next day, 22nd, at a village called Alvelade, only three miles from Lisbon, a large number of English soldiers were poisoned, either by the bad water from a well, or, as some said, by the honey which they had found in the houses. It was Alvelade that Don Antonio lodged at the house of a friend, Juan Luis Estabas Ferreira de Gama. His friend was absent but his wife Dona Maria was at home. This was unexpected because Don Antonio had been told that she was in hiding at Torres Vedra, for safety's sake he took her and her son, Francisco, with him and back to England. When the English arrived at Alvelade, Count de Fuentes, with the main body of Spaniards, was at Alcantara, a mile or so nearer Lisbon to the west.

At eleven o'clock at night Essex and Sir Roger Williams left the camp with 1,000 men to lie in ambush near Lisbon. When they came near to the city walls a few of them began banging on the gates, trying to alarm those inside into provoking the Spanish to make a sally. But the attempted deception was too transparent and the only results were that a few men were shot and everyone had a sleepless night.

The Spanish sneered that on its way to Lisbon the army had taken only one "small miserable village," garrisoned by a few horse who fled after only a slight resistance, so allowing the people to welcome Don Antonio.

Cardinal-Archduke Albert hastily summoned a council of war at Alcantara near Lisbon, where all the troops were to muster and urged his officers at last to make a stand at once before the English could co-operate with their friends within the city walls. De Fuentes and the other Spanish commanders were of the same opinion, but the Portuguese Colonel, Fernando de Castro, made a speech pointing out that the English were short of stores, cut off from their base, and weakened by sickness and short commons.

He is reported to have said, "Let us fall back into the city and conquer them by hunger and delay. Behind our walls they will be powerless to injure us, whilst we can draw abundant supplies from across the river, and they cannot blockade us even by and with less than 40,000 men." This exactly suited the other Portuguese, who, according to the Spanish, were never comfortable unless they had a good thick wall between themselves and their enemies. The opinion of the Spanish officers was overborne and the defending force entered the gates of Lisbon on Corpus Christi day, to the ringing of bells and the, more or less, sincere rejoicing of the population.

Lisbon in the late 16th century

Lisbon – Part 1

The Spanish, who had eventually accepted that nothing could be done about the defence of the distant Azores, at long last distributed troops along the Iberian coast and then concentrated on the defence of Lisbon. 3,000 Spanish troops and 400 cavalry were encamped at the town of Cascais on the north side of the estuary and at other strategic points nearby.

When it became evident after the landing at Peniche that the attack was targeted on Lisbon, an elaborate assumption was made that the English intended to make an attack from the landward side, firstly by taking the two castles at the harbour mouth to allow the fleet to enter, and then to make a combined attack by land and sea. That it was not so much the aim of the English, led by Don Antonio, Drake and Norris, to take the city by themselves, because their numbers were known to be insufficient to take a whole city without other support, but to throw Lisbon and its occupying force of Spaniards into confusion. The citizens would have the opportunity to revolt in the name of Don Antonio and open the gates for the English to march in.

Had the attack been weeks earlier it might have worked, but it was too late, ample warning had been given by the time-consuming attack on Coruna and the march from Peniche, for the Spanish to do all they could to remove the potential leaders from the Portuguese nobility, and demoralise the masses to the point where they were fairly confident that no uprising would take place. Even so, the Spanish left nothing to chance in their preparations for defence. At the mouth of the River Tagus there were three towers, to which another two had been added nearer the capital, and a great chain had been stretched across the river between them, and it was ensured that they were well garrisoned with troops and provisions. The Portuguese were armed and put under the command of three colonels, but they were well dispersed so that in any event of rebellion they could not cause trouble.

Inside the capital there was intense excitement. The native inhabitants, with a lively recollection of the sacking of the city years earlier by the Duke of Alba, fled to the other side of the Tagus, notwithstanding the strict orders of the viceroy, Cardinal-Archduke Albert, Philip's nephew, to the contrary. Provisions and munitions of war were hastily sent from Spain, and the people were aware that the Prior Don Ernando de Toledo was already on the move, slowly bringing such troops as he could muster for the relief of Lisbon, while the castles and walls of the city were put into a state of defence. The Spanish, who were few in number and intensely hated by the townsfolk, knew that in a fight the brunt of it would fall on them, and that the Portuguese, even though they might not help the enemy, and this was by no means certain, would not raise a finger to support King Philip.

However, Don Antonio did have supporters inside the walls, and the Spanish-controlled government knew of individuals who "by money or by correspondence" were in contact with him. Priests, who almost to a man were his strongest adherents, went from house to house whispering among other things, that the English were not, after all, such bad people, that there were many Catholics amongst them who were better Christians than the Spanish themselves. They attempted to influence the well-to-do by telling them that as soon as their native king was on the throne their wealth would increase enormously, and the poor were told subtly that "fishing in troubled waters was profitable to the fisherman."

To counter this, Cardinal-Archduke Albert, knowing the people with whom he had to deal, had established a veritable reign of terror, and sacrificed without mercy, and often without evidence, every person who was even suspected of open sympathy with the invaders. It was believed by the Spaniards in Lisbon and in far-off Madrid that the people of Lisbon had tacitly agreed to open the gates to Don Antonio and to massacre the Spaniards on his approach. Some Portuguese nobles had left the Archduke on the first landing of Don Antonio, but, finding that most of their order had been terrorised into quiescence, returned to Lisbon and tendered their submission. Many of the Portuguese 'traitors' were captured and the chief ones were executed, they were at once beheaded or imprisoned, and the rest became more slavish than ever in their professions of attachment to the Archduke. But not all Portuguese nobles were under suspicion; the loyalty of many was not questioned. They knew which side their bread was buttered.

The fate of one Portuguese noble who was a strong supporter of Don Antonio is known; Emanuel Gomez de Vas, a man "of vast and famous riches," had been a long time in correspondence with Don Antonio had to flee to Africa, his property was confiscated and his sons were proclaimed as rebels.

Terrible stories were deliberately circulated about the "impious abominations" of the English heretics, and the dreadful fate that awaited all Catholics if the invader succeeded, until, "there was not even a loafer on the quay who did not know he would be cast out or ruined if the English came." But all this was not enough to make the people willing to fight for the cause of their Spanish overlords. The exodus from the city continued, under cover of night the people stole across the River Tagus by thousands, with the result that a boat whose usual freight was two ducats could not be hired for less than fifty, while a bullock-cart and bullocks which could be bought outright in normal times for fifty ducats now charged sixty for a single journey to Aldea Gallega, on the south side of the Tagus. And when the refugees reached the country the people there harassed them and preyed on them until they were feared more than the English enemy. The scandal became so great that the Archduke had to interfere and check the rapacity.

Under some excuse or another every Portuguese was anxious to get away and leave the fighting to be done by someone else. This was not because ordinary Portuguese people were not cowards or traitors, but simply because they could not rise without the organisation and leadership of their own nobles. Added to this was the fact that they had been terrorised and made powerless by the harsh repressive methods implemented by the Archduke.

The Spaniards themselves made no secret of their contempt for the "white-livered Lisbonenses," and used abusive language when discussing them. A Portuguese, who had remained in the city and was tolerated but may or may not have been trusted, was present during these days and recalled an example of the attitude of Spanish toward the citizens of Lisbon. "On the morning that the enemy fled I went up to the castle to get some things of mine out of my boxes which I had left there in the rooms of one of the officers, where I had determined to await my fate if things came to the worst. As I was on my way down to the palace again the rumour spread that the enemy was retreating, whereupon some soldiers ascended the watchtower to enjoy the sight. I asked them when they returned if the good news were true that the enemy was really flying, and one of them answered roughly that they who were flying were not the enemy but those who still stay in Lisbon. To which I answered him not a word but God be with ye."

By terrorism imposed with energy and promptness the Archduke had at length got the city of Lisbon into a state of defence against the certain enemy without and the probable enemy within, for instance, the city water-tanks were locked and water was brought from outside, so as to store as much as possible for the coming siege. The Spanish residents formed themselves into a bodyguard of 150 men, "very smart and well-armed," and the German and Flemish communities in the city offered two hundred arquebussiers in good order, while many of the Portuguese gentry slept in the corridors of the palace, ostensibly to protect the Archduke in the hour of need but perhaps also to save themselves by demonstrating their own loyalty.

Four colonels were appointed to organise bands of inhabitants for the defence of the city, and a renowned sea-captain, Matias de Alburquerque, took charge of the twelve war galleys that were at anchor in the Tagus, and he armed thirty merchant ships that were lying in the harbour. The defensive works around the city were divided into sections and allocated to the command of tried and trusted officers. Most of the houses adjoining the walls had been blown up to remove cover for the attackers and give a clear field of fire.

Defence of the river front being mainly entrusted to Portuguese, who considered their post the most exposed and threatened, because they were without walls to protect them along the quay side. But the Spanish made no secret of the fact that they were placed there because no attack was expected from the river. The quarters of St. Catalina, San Antonio, and San Roque, facing the north and west, from where the English advance was expected, were to be most strongly guarded, and almost entirely by Spaniards.

The atmosphere was tense and uncertain. The local citizens were distracted and divided; judges and magistrates had abandoned their posts, shopkeepers had deserted their stores, there were frequent, almost incessant, incendiary fires, and pillage was rife. The Archduke alone kept his head, but even he was not free from the threat of attack, for more than one attempt was made to assassinate some of his chief officers.

On one occasion a large number of men were caught deserting their posts and trying to escape by boat to the other side of the Tagus. When they were brought to the Archduke for punishment he said if they were too cowardly to fight in defence of their God and their fatherland they were useless to him and they could go. This he knew, that even the Castilian women would mount the walls and fight with stones, if need be, in such a cause. The Archduke required all his firmness and nerve, for one sign of weakness from him and his handful of Spaniards would have given heart to the Portuguese inside and outside the walls who were thirsting for their blood.

One estimate was that three quarters of the Portuguese population of Lisbon had fled or were in hiding, while the rest were in Spanish pay or were under suspicion and had to be watched day and night.

News came daily from English prisoners and others of the approach of King Don Antonio and watched as they were, and few in numbers, their hopes were still high, and amongst themselves their speech grew bolder and they plotted together how they would deal with the hated Spanish when the English deliverers came.

A rumour went around that the city would be surrendered to the invader on the day of Corpus Christi, that not a Spaniard was to be left alive, and much more to the same effect. But when the occasion appeared to arise, when a few English prisoners were being brought in, there was a panic that the invaders had entered the city and people went into hiding instead of manning their posts, and the few Spanish guards that remained had to drag them out of cellars and lofts by force, kicking them and cuffing them, calling them cowards for not helping the defenders.

Once, on a false alarm, the Count de Fuentes was sent out of the city with every man who could be spared to Oeiras, five miles off on the road to Cascais, where it was expected the enemy would pass; but the English were on their way by Torres Vedras, and Fuentes had to hurry back into Lisbon again the same day to avoid the risk of being cut off and the gates being shut against him.

The Cardinal-Archduke set a good personal example to his troops by going to any part that was threatened encouraging the defenders to do their best, and the Spanish garrison was heartened to an extent by the knowledge that their commander, the great Don Ernando, was on his way, but nevertheless there was still a great deal of anxiety. Quite when Don Ernando could be expected to arrive could not be told. He had left Zamora to the north-west of Madrid and was on his way, marching towards to the town of Valencia de Alcantara near the border, where all the troops were to muster, which is not to be confused with Alcantara to the west of Lisbon. When everything was ready there would be a total of 11,000 or 12,000 Spanish troops and 600 horse. But all the time there was the worry that progress was so slow that even when he reached Alcantara it would be 150 miles and several days march away from Lisbon. Would his army arrive in time to be of assistance?

A letter written by Don Francisco Odonte, the adjutant-general in Lisbon, on the day following the arrival of the English forces before the walls, gives a vivid description of the state of affairs there at the time wrote that, "for those who have shown their colours during the last three days, and that without a blush, are simply infinite," and concluded, "All the aldermen of the city are against us but two, the rest are all in hiding, and some have even supplied Don Antonio's troops, with as little shamefacedness as if they had come from England with him. In this quarter of the city there is not a man left. Some have fled across the river, some are hidden, some have joined Don Antonio. The troops under the four colonels publicly declare they will not fight. Don Antonio was certain the moment he appeared the city would rise, and on this account we are in great alarm and have passed a very bad night. God help us!"

The men who had come on board Drake's ships that landed at Cascais, were joined at Sintra to the west of Lisbon by the 4,000 who had marched with Don Antonio from Peniche. On their way south, according to an English commentator, these men had marched every day in excellent order, given the constraints imposed on them, and had entrenched themselves every night. It was anticipated that the army would first attack the two castles near the capital and open the way for the fleet to sail to Lisbon, so throwing the city into confusion, when, it was hoped, the people would rise in support of Don Antonio. Drake's intention originally was assist this by setting two ships on fire in front of the castle of San Gian so that the whole fleet would enter the harbour unseen through the smoke.

The Count of Fuentes came out on the road to Cascais from Lisbon with his infantry to confront the English, his army consisting of 2,000 Spaniards and 8,000 Portuguese, and formed a camp at Alcantara about a mile and a half from the city, the place where Don Antonio has been defeated in 1580. But he found his men so unwilling to march and so inclined to Don Antonio that during the night the Portuguese contingent dwindled to 2,000. The Count realised that these deserters would not be coerced to rejoin. Then the Cardinal, who had also come out to pitch his camp three miles away, warned him that many plots in favour of Don Antonio had been discovered in the city, and so after a few days of due consideration they both withdrew without even having seen the English. The

Count de Fuentes returned and re-entered the city on the Feast of Corpus Christi and settled down to defend the city from behind the city walls and strengthen them until Don Ernando and his army arrived.

After a rapid march of fifteen miles from Cascais to within three miles of Lisbon, the English army, with night coming on, occupied the suburbs of Santa Caterina and San Antonio. Here they took up their quarters and started to plan an attack on the fortifications, which were old and weak.

The next day, on the 3rd of June, the defenders came out to harass them with a sortie led by Don Sancho Bravo and a company of arquebusiers, and Captain Gasparo of Alcaron with two companies of light horse, who spent the day skirmishing outside the city walls. Here "the English awaited the attack right merrily, and the engagement was fought with courage." In one incident, Sancho Brava's lieutenant, Conteas, was killed, but only, according the Spanish sources, after slaying many English with his own hands, in revenge for which the English cut him into pieces.

At first the English were repulsed, the Spaniards taking twenty-five or thirty English prisoners who were immediately put to row in the galleys. An observer of this commented, "If they (the Spanish army) would only do the same by all those who are really fighting us while feigning to be friends (meaning the Portuguese in the city and in general), they might man more galleys than are to be found in all Christendom." It was noticeable that no Portuguese had come forward to offer their services in the Spanish cause.

Despite this setback, that afternoon the English army continued to advance towards Lisbon in two divisions, not sacking any village, in the anticipation that the people would open the city gates for them and welcome their new king. Don Antonio had, after all, promised to restore their old liberties and ensure them of the removal and "the destruction of the Castilian (Spanish) yoke."

Unusually, once more for an army on the march, the troops did not indulge in plunder, but probably only because everything that could be carried had been already carried into the city, and that which could not be removed in the time available was burned to prevent it falling into their hands.

The news of the English advance had prompted the Cardinal Archduke to give orders for a review of all arms, to close all the gates and sally ports and place garrisons at every point. The government of the city passed that first night in a state of great alarm. The governor was convinced that any sign of weakness the city would be lost, he made a show of bravery, going about rallying the defenders to the point that supporters of Don Antonio did not dare show themselves, a situation for the Spanish that was improving all the time. The Spanish soldiers were then deployed, some to the damaged wall, while the rest were divided into three divisions, one at the Palace Square, another at the Rosseo, and the third at the Enfanci.

All this led to the Spanish defenders gaining in confidence to repel the invaders. The poor physical condition of the English on had been noticed their arrival, and the several weeks gained for the city's defenders by English delays had given them time to prepare. There was the hope that, so long as they could hold out and the English failed to take the city, the advancing Spanish army would defeat the besiegers and inflict damage on them during their withdrawal back to the fleet.

During the day the Spanish were reinforced by 600 men, all veteran Spanish, who arrived from Oporto in the north, while it was known that the Duke of Feria was on his way with a large number of horsemen and arquebusiers. His 2,500 troops with six companies of horse were expected on the 4th.

With regard to the English army, the remainder of the day, now that the main body had come up, was spent in quartering the men around the suburbs of the city and constructing entrenched camps that were protected by breastworks made of wine pipes filled with earth.

Finally Norris's army, tired with their six days' march and their labour in the trenches, passed their first night before Lisbon in such peace as the besieged would allow them. That night there was a skirmish in the suburb of San Antonio in which it was believed that the English lost 150 men and the defenders about fifteen or twenty arquebussiers and four or five men-at-arms because they could not fight as well in the street as in the open country.

Spanish propagandists put about that, "Lisbon feasted and welcomed its defenders, while poor Don Antonio, we are told, at Alvelade, just outside, had not a fowl or even a loaf of rye bread to eat. You may guess how he is hated by the Portuguese that he being so near his native Lisbon not even a costermonger or a clown dared to send him a meal, while we in the city had plenty."

By early next morning the English had completed their investment of the city and they were assessing the old and weak fortifications in preparation of an assault, the walls were also being reconnoitred for a secret gate though which to enter, or an unguarded gate, of which there was little hope, the public gates being shut and guarded, and all the time the English soldiers were being harassed by musket fire from the garrison high on the city walls.

It soon became obvious that the people of Lisbon had not risen immediately. Unknown to the English this was due to "the prudence and calmness" of his Highness the Prince Cardinal who had 'pacified' the city, weeding out any sympathisers among the inhabitants and the garrison and thoroughly punishing them as a deterrent as a warning to the citizens. The ultimate deterrent came when one man was beheaded. As a result the city was quiet.

But the English did not sleep tranquilly. During the early hours of the morning of the 4th June Don Garcia Bravo, with 100 or 500 Spanish troops, arrived in Lisbon from Oporto. Again according to Spanish sources, they were hungry, ragged and weary, but eager to meet the foe, and they barely gave themselves time to snatch a hurried meal before sallying out from the gate of San Anton and up the hill to the quarters of Colonel Brett in the farm of Andres Soares.

Another force came at the same time from the gate of Santa Catalina and forced Brett's trenches from that side. Above them were the long rows of windows of the monastery of San Roque on the hill that were lined by Spanish musketeers who kept up a deadly fire on the English, while two of the great guns of the castle were brought to bear upon one exposed side of the invaders' camp. The attack was made before dawn, and Brett had hardly time to muster his men in the darkness and confusion, when a cannon-shot from the walls laid him low. Captain Carsey and Captain Carr were mortally wounded and 200 other officers and men were slain. The rest of the English forces were aroused and came to the rescue under Colonel Lane and Colonel Medkirk and put the Spaniards "to a sodain fowle retreate, insomuch as the Earle of Essex had the chase of them even to the gates of the High towne, wherein they left behind them many of their best commanders."

A body of Spanish horse, sallying forth from the gates of San Anton to support their comrades, met them in full retreat in a narrow lane and unwillingly trampled them down so adding to the confusion, which was completed by a flank charge upon the struggling mass by Yorke's cavalry. The English report claimed that the Spanish loss tripled that of the English, but on the Spanish side the report was that they had only twenty-five killed and forty wounded. A Portuguese chronicler tried to account for the heavy loss of wounded by accusing the English of using poisoned bullets.

By the end of the day the Spanish claimed that the English had lost 400 men as well as the twenty-five prisoners. An English colonel had died and five officers and many men, with "an infinity" who were wounded. On account of this, and because the cavalry of Don Sancho Brava and others harassed them continually, giving them much to do, the English retired to their quarters.

That night the defending troops gave them another attack, an *incamisata* (a shirt sleeve), attack in which, the Spanish claimed, many English were slain and the rest thrown into confusion. In all the skirmishes, the Spaniards claimed, the English had the worst of it, always losing men.

But what of Don Antonio all this time? He was lodged at the house of the Duke d'Avero, from where he had gone to the Apostolic College at the Teatines, to confess his sins and receive many visits from "Portuguese Jews and other low folk," according to rather biased Spanish sources.

Although most of the suburban houses adjoining the walls had been blown up by the defending Spanish, the monastery of the Trinidade, down the hill towards the river, still remained. The prior was understood to be in favour of Don Antonio, as were nearly all churchmen, and one of the few nobles with Don Antonio, Ruy Diaz de Lobo, a great noble and a rich gentleman of Lisbon, undertook to negotiate with him to admit the English to the city through the monastery garden. By the aid of two sympathetic monks he obtained access to the prior, but they had been won over by the Spaniards and informed on Ruy Diazlovo, who was arrested and found to be in possession of a letter, secret correspondence with Don Antonio.

When Sir Roger Williams and his men approached the monastery in expectation of a friendly reception, they were received with a shower of harquebus balls, and fell back. A few hours later the heads of Ruy Diaz de Lobo and the two monks were seen impaled on three poles on the great quay.

During the day a friar who was under suspicion was arrested and his head cut off on the spot. He was taking 18,000 ducats to Don Antonio. Even in the very headquarters of Spanish Don Antonio had his sympathisers; a lieutenant of the antechamber of the Prince Cardinal, Louis Gonzales, who had tried to desert to Don Antonio during the sortie was arrested. On him were found letters from Don Antonio. He was also beheaded. If these men had actually been guilty it meant that Don Antonio would have been informed of Spanish proceedings in Lisbon for years past.

The day after this the English bribed a Portuguese captain who was in charge of the city wall at the point nearest to the river to let them pass round it at low tide, but spies informed the Archduke and the English found their ally replaced by a Spaniard with a strong force, who sent them flying back again.

And yet the Spanish were alarmed at just how many supporters of Don Antonio had shown themselves during the first three days of the siege despite all their deterrents, while no one had come forward to support the government of the occupation. Within the army itself some troops had not been afraid to declare in public that they would not fight. There was also news that Don Antonio had been supplied with provisions and munitions while the city had only managed to get a supply of fifty or sixty cows brought in by a squadron from the quarter of San Rocco.

All the magistrates except two had gone into hiding and some were even sending supplies to Don Antonio, "with as little shamefacedness as though they had come with him from England." In one quarter of the city there was reported to be not a man left, many had fled across the river, some had hidden and some had joined Don Antonio.

The fate of the whole English enterprise was now in the balance, the outcome of the siege was in the hands of the people. If the people rose and rebelled, then the siege would be successful, Don Antonio and the English would be successful, if they did not, then the siege would fail and the English did not have sufficient strength in numbers to attack the main cities in the region.

Lisbon – Part 2

If the enterprise was ever to succeed this was the moment. The English were more numerous as regards men bearing arms, but they had come upon their wild-goose chase without any battering artillery or proper appliances for a siege, while the Spaniards were behind strong walls, with unlimited sources of supply from the river front across the Tagus. Norris, on the other hand, was short of supplies, with fifteen miles of defensible country between him and Cascais, the point where the fleet was to await him. The advantage, therefore, was clearly on the side of besieged, but for one element of the disaffection of Lisbon itself from within, and in this lay Don Antonio's last chance.

The English remained for four days without making any assault, only awaiting the success of the many plots which they had made with the Portuguese to admit them. They skirmished around the city but the Spanish claimed they were defeated each on each occasion.

The army was estimated to be between 12,000 and 15,000 strong with 400 horse and "some pieces of artillery," described dismissively as if they posed no great threat. Don Antonio was nominally in supreme command but in reality John Norris was the acting commander.

Three days went by with the city of Lisbon under siege and in constant skirmishes from the defenders by day and night, while Norris was chafing and helpless. The fatal mistake that had been made in leaving the fleet was now apparent. The time, too, they had lost at Coruna was irreparable. The loss of men in the English camp from sickness and wounds was terrible, supplies and munitions were desperately short, there was no medical aid or transport for the sick and disabled, whilst the Portuguese in Lisbon, from whom everything had been hoped, still made no sign of revolt. All the while, Fernando de Toledo was approaching with relief for the city, his 2,500 men and six companies of horse were expected any day. The first dismay in Spain had now given way to desperate energy.

From the lack of movement within the city, Don Antonio realised that the people were not going to rise in his support and he knew that relief for them was expected, so on the 5th of June he withdrew from the city walls between half a mile and a mile away towards the sea, where the troops entrenched themselves strongly and kept quiet.

Among the defenders, however, there was still a cause for concern. Their munitions and provisions were stored in the suburbs that were in English possession, not having had time to remove them, they had been destroyed by the government to prevent them falling into enemy hands. Another factor was that the garrison was for the most part Portuguese and therefore not to be completely trusted either to obey or to stand and fight. This had already been proved when the Count Fuentes made his sortie with the company of Portuguese infantry and found them so unwilling to march and so sympathetic to Don Antonio that he had had to return without even having seen the enemy.

Don Antonio was believed to be strengthening his position all the time. By 6th June in Lisbon more conspiracies to support him had been discovered and the leaders imprisoned, having been informed upon by one of Philip's spies in Don Antonio's court, which one is not known for certain, but it was probably Diego Rodriguez, his treasurer, a Portuguese noble who had been with Don Antonio but escaped at Coruna and gone to King Philip. However, in the main the Portuguese nobility were judged to be thoroughly loyal to Spain and that it was only the common people who found cause with Don Antonio. Even so, all correspondence continued to be opened and read, including even some of the King Philip's dispatches.

Meanwhile, Drake remained at Cascais, with the English fleet, which led the Spanish to surmise correctly that he would not come at all to the harbour at Lisbon. Part of the fleet, consisting of "many ships", was sent to Morocco to bring the hoped-for troop reinforcements from Al-Mansur, who had 30,000 horse for Don Antonio. They were ready to embark when Al-Mansur became alarmed for the safety of his son, Muley Moluk, who was with his step-father Hassan Pasha, and he therefore refrained from assisting the English and furthermore sent letters to reassure King Philip that he did not wish to break off their friendly relations. Even with the hovering threat of the Turkish fleet, this gave King Philip confidence that Drake's hopes for more troops would almost certainly be refused. Philip was now confident that the English expedition would be a failure and he continued to collect money and building ships in preparation for another attack on England.

Sir Francis Drake, commander of the English Armada

The Spanish knew that Elizabeth had an agent at the shereef's court but regardless of this it was reasonable to assume that Drake would receive only a refusal or some protracted promises. However, Philip remained on guard, not trusting either Drake or Al-Mansur. In the background there was still the fear that a fleet of twenty-two galleys of Hizir Pasha of Algiers and twelve of Murad III, the sultan of Turkey, would intervene on Don Antonio's behalf. It was thought that King Henry of France had suggested this to Hizir Pasha in order to annoy the Philip, who at the time was being harried by the English on the west and the Algerians on the east.

For King Philip, the whole English expedition was only one of several affairs of state to be dealt with, and all the while, regardless of the English invasion, he was preparing for another Armada against England to sail in March the next year.

As the days went by, Don Antonio, although he put a brave face on the matter, was becoming despondent. He looked in vain for the general rising in his favour from then populace, and for the promised nobles who never came, and hour by hour the prospect of success darkened. For the first two days after the withdrawal he had lodged in the rear of the English camp, outside Santa Catalina, but on the third day, he had begun to fear for his safety, and, wearied of low fare and the sound of musketry, sought refuge in the house of Juan Luis Estabas Ferreira da Gama, a Portuguese gentleman on the road to Cascais. But he was driven away and barely escaped capture, and after that he stayed with the English force.

Among the English nobles, the Earl of Essex, young, inexperienced, hot-headed, was for assaulting all sorts of impossible places with pike and musket ball, but Norris knew better, and sadly acknowledged to himself that the expedition had failed.

From Cascais, Drake and the fleet cruised about to take everything he could lay hands on in the form of prizes. He had cast anchor on the very day twelvemonth that the great Armada had first sailed out of Lisbon, and the superstitious people of the capital saw omens in this coincidence. Everyone in Lisbon by this time feared that he would sail up the river and enter the harbour; and such was the dread of his name that if he had done so he might have turned the tide of victory. But his advice had been rejected, and he would not venture under the guns of the forts with an under-manned fleet and no soldiers. So he remained at Cascais and left Norris to get out of the hobble as best he could.

When he arrived at Cascais Drake had found the town almost abandoned, the citizens had fled in terror at his name. In the fortress of the town the commander, Cardenas, "a great gentleman," claimed he was deceived by a monk, or, as he said later in his defence, the devil in disguise of one, into the belief that Lisbon had fallen, so accordingly he gave up the fortress, and himself took to flight.

The Spanish account stated that Cardenas was an adherent of Don Antonio, and that only a show of compulsion had been made before he surrendered the fortress. The result in any case was all the same to Cardenas, for the head of the "great gentleman" soon afterwards adorned one of the Archduke's poles on the quay at Lisbon.

Drake had therefore established himself without difficulty at Cascais, and patiently awaited the result of the land attack on Lisbon. Their fleet lay at the bar of the river, and prevented all egress or ingress to any shipping; it intended to sail in the moment Lisbon showed signs of suffering want.

If the English outside the walls of the capital were in a bad way, the small force of steadfast Spaniards inside were not much better. They knew that the Portuguese citizens around them were hourly watching for an opportunity to cut their throats and let in the native pretender. Panics of treason and treachery were an hourly occurrence, and on several occasions only the coolness of the Cardinal-Archduke averted disaster. Every day men of the best blood of Portugal, often taken from the immediate surrounding of the Archduke, were seized for assumed treason, the policy being to deprive the disaffected populace of native leaders. To further terrorise the citizens and prevent them from plucking up courage to open the gates, a great review of all the Spanish troops was held in an open space where the enemy as well as the wavering townsfolk could see them.

The boldness and firmness of the Spanish had won the day. The next morning Norris called his colonels together to seek their advice and consult with Don Antonio. He said that as the besieged stood firm and the populace was making no move, the English force must have artillery and munitions if they were to succeed. He asked their opinion as to whether he should wait for Don Antonio's forces, which had not appeared and meanwhile send a detachment to Cascais for munitions, or else raise the siege altogether. Many of them were for sending 3,000 men to Cascais immediately.

They had given the enemy a good drubbing, they said, and they would not appear again; but Norris had lost hope in Portuguese promises and was not quite so contemptuous of the Spanish as some of them, so he decided that he would wait only one day more from Don Antonio's levies. If 3,000 came in that night he would send a like number of English to Cascais for the munitions, otherwise he would raise the siege and leave before daybreak. Don Antonio asked for a few days' grace; given nine days he believed all Portugal would acclaim him; Lisbon was wavering already and would turn the scale. But all his pleas were in vain; before dawn the English army was mustered and made ready for the march. Essex was disgusted at the turn things had taken, and went up to the principal gate (he and Williams being the last men to leave) and broke his lance against it, crying out that if there was any within who would come out and have a bout with him in honour of his mistress let him come, and he gave them all the lie to their teeth. And then he turned away and followed the army, no doubt much relieved that no one had come forward to answer his challenge.

During the day that Norris was awaiting the arrival of Don Antonio's troops, the English soldiers had not left their trenches and the defenders feared that some deep design lay behind this. Were they mining under the city walls, or could Drake now be sending up some heavy guns? So when the dawn of the 6th June showed that the main body of the English, unnoticed by the Count de Fuentes, was already on its way to Cascais, the count still doubted whether it was not all a feint to draw him out from the shelter of the walls, and peremptorily refused permission to Count Villa Dorta's request to follow them up and engage with them.

In spite of the count's refusal, a few horse did go after the enemy, killing a few stragglers, so leading the Spanish to crow that if all their troops had marched out of Lisbon not one man of the English army would have escaped alive. But the reality of the Spanish situation was that, up to this moment, not a single soldier had arrived to relieve the city and so the Count of Fuentes, for the sake of Lisbon, for the sake of the Cardinal's personal safety and because he knew that the Portuguese troops were not to be trusted, did not dare to leave the city and take the field with the few troops on whom he could actually rely, which amounted to fewer than 1,500 men. This, as it turned out was a wise decision, because soon afterwards 2,000 Portuguese sent by the Duke of Braganza and 800 sent by the Duke of Feria arrived.

The English marched off some seven or eight miles. The way of their retreat lay along the shore of the Tagus estuary, but to avoid the fire of the galleys which followed their movements they chose the rough by-paths wherever possible. By now undisciplined, sick, and starving, they wandered and struggled on as best they could, 400 at least of the stragglers and sick being killed or captured by Villa Dorta, who hung upon the rear, notwithstanding his chief's prohibition. Later in the day Fuentes so far conquered his doubts as to lead his army out to Viera, half way to Cascais, but he had barely sighted the enemy than some rumour or suspicion reached him of an intended rising in Lisbon during his absence, and he hurried back again to the city.

During all this activity, the following incident occurred. Alvaro Souza, the captain of King Philip's Portuguese guard, with five companions, accompanied Sancho Bravo, who took out a force to harry the English on their way to Cascais. Souza straggled and was captured by Spanish soldiers, who did not know him. They were near the castle of San Gian at the mouth of Lisbon harbour and knowing that Pero Venegas, the commandant, was a friend of his father, Souza sent a message to him begging him to answer for his loyalty. Venegas declined to reply, and Souza was led off under arrest.

On the way he met the famous Alvaro de Bazan going to his galleys. He was a friend, and Souza appealed to him to stand by him and his companions, "but he answered coldly that he knew him not, nor was this a time to recognise anyone." He had, he said, recently answered for some Portuguese hidalgos in the palace, and a few hours afterwards they had been arrested for treason.

The effects of the siege in the suburbs of Lisbon were minimal, the English had not sacked or burnt or destroyed any buildings, or even damaged the churches, which was thought miraculous. There had been little looting, but this might have been due mainly to the fact that the best things had already been removed, and the Count had already stripped all provisions from the suburbs, he had ordered the ordnance to be thrown into the river any warehouses in which there were victuals to be set on fire, and all the wine to be poured away.

During the time the English army had been camped near the walls, and in the retreat to Cascais, 500 men in total were killed and over 50 taken prisoner. On their side the Spanish claimed that only 25 were lost and two officers wounded. How reliable these figures are is anyone's guess.

In the end, Drake's fleet, which should have moved up the River Tagus to alter the course of the siege, remained at its mouth. The besieging force under Don Antonio and Sir John Norris lacked the appropriate arms and equipment, while the Portuguese themselves did nothing to help their perceived rightful king. Don Antonio, King Antonio, had found little response from his own countrymen, some of whom, it was believed, had not risen because their hatred of the invading English heretics was even stronger than their hatred of Spanish. As a result, Norris had had no choice but to withdraw his disease-ridden and demoralised army. Eventually the army reached Cascais, where the fleet, the English Armada, lay, to prepare for its departure for home and the wrath of Queen Elizabeth.

Cascais

Drake and Norris, the commanders of what had become a great embarrassment, were now in Cascais, beginning to wonder how to put themselves right with their angry queen, who continued to send furious messages about their disobedience and about Essex and Sir Roger Williams. On the 12th of June they wrote from Cascais a full count of all that had happened in the best light they could devise, saying that they knew not what to do unless supplies came at once from England. Everybody was terribly seasick, they said, and well-nigh starving.

On 1st June it had been reported that "They are so reduced by the heat of the weather that they are not now above 4,000 fighting men. They were ready to sail to Cadiz or Barbary to be revictualled, or else return by the Spanish coast. They found biscuit and corn at Lisbon sufficient for 40,000 men for one year and had taken 60 or 80 sail of Easterlings laden with stores."

During the day the English troops had managed to cover fifteen or sixteen weary miles over rough ground to Cascais with Villa Dorta's troops harassing their flank and rear, and late in the evening they marched into Cascais.

On their way, if the Earl of Essex was rash and headstrong, he proved he was also chivalrous. Wingfield/Pricket wrote: "He for money hired men to carrie sick and hurt upon pikes (for want of waggons) and hee (whose true virtue and nobilitie, as it dooth in all other his actions appear so did it very much in this) threw his owne stuffe, I mean apparell and necessaries from his owne carriages, and let them be left by the way, to put hurt and sick men upon them in this march."

It is quite likely that the meeting between Drake and Norris was not very cordial. The officers threw the whole blame for failure upon Drake for not coming up the river to support them before Lisbon; the sailors on the other hand saying that the march overland was against Drake's advice, and that his ships, without men-at-arms to defend them or artillery to fire the guns, would have been at the mercy of the enemy. At all events, it was clear that they had failed in two of the three objects of the voyage – namely, to burn the King of Spain's ships and restore Don Antonio. The only one aim remained was to take the islands of the Azores.

Among them the 500 men lost in the retreat from Lisbon a colonel was killed by peasants who also chased the enemy for some time. But by withdrawing they had hoped, as Count de Fuentes suspected, that the defending troops would be drawn after them and so encourage the inhabitants of the city at last to rise up. But this did not succeed.

The English took up a position at Cascais with the fleet on their front and both flanks entrenched and began to bombard the town with five pieces of heavy artillery. They attacked and took a small weak fortress there, mainly because of the nuisance it might cause than a thing of value, without even having to threaten it with cannonfire. The castle was found to have been garrisoned by 400 soldiers, and seven good pieces of artillery, eleven barrels of gunpowder, and 150 quintals of biscuits, pork and tunny sausage. The Spanish did not know whether it was weakness or cowardice that made the fortress surrender, but in any case the commander was arrested afterwards and taken to Lisbon for punishment, which was to be condemned to death, unless King Philip pardoned him. It was uncertain from the Spanish point of view whether the enemy were waiting to embark or waiting for reinforcements from Africa. Whatever the plan, more guns had been brought ashore, perhaps with the intention of holding on and still being able to wreak havoc in the country.

Soon afterwards six vessels came into the harbour laden with corn for German merchants, although they were sailing under a safe conduct from Elizabeth, the English seized them. However, the Count of Fuentes had already broken the mills of Cintra and of Cascais so that the enemy could not make use of them and provisions began to run short.

Not everyone had lost faith in Don Antonio, about 25 Portuguese gentlemen, those who had not much to lose, but were well armed and fully equipped, had joined him, and also some 400 of the ordinary people. He was also visited by faithful priests and friars.

The Spaniards in believing that if the English held Cascais they might still be able to wreak havoc in Portugal so would not let a man out of the castle in Lisbon, without instantly charging them, they drove back 1,000 musketeers who had gone out to forage but they claimed that Don Ernando drove them out.

With the enemy soldiers gone from the gates of Lisbon and cornered in Cascais, the Spanish were able to gather their forces. Don Alonzo de Vargas and the Duke of Braganza collected a large body of cavalry and while they were doing this, bad weather forced the fleet to retire to Peniche and the Count of Fuentes was able to put his troops between the fleet and Don Antonio's army.

The fleet returned and the English began to embark on the 13th of July, being forced to leave behind some 400 Portuguese due to lack of provisions, so it was claimed. The Spanish also claimed that they took on board the sick and wounded and the clergy but landed them all again the next day, except a few people of importance, taking from them everything they possessed and beating them with sticks.

They took the artillery out of Cascais to be put back on board ship and, again due to want of provisions, left only one more or less sacrificial company of 300 English and 400 Portuguese in the town which was given over to the sack. It was supposed that many of the English stayed behind of their own accord and voluntarily and converted to Catholicism.

Don Antonio, Drake and Norris could not help but be aware that the army was visibly wasting away through illness, wounds and death, and that the Portuguese people had not risen up as expected and as promised. The English army suffered the loss of about half its complement through disease, desertion and battles. A Flemish volunteer, reckoned by Wingfield/Pricket to be "a competent judge," calculated that between Corunna and Lisbon, skirmishes and sickness, the English had lost 5,000 men.

In their preparations for departure the ships took water on board and cleared the whole district of cattle and made some kind of biscuit until the supply of grist failed.

On the 14th June Don Antonio embarked, having reluctantly abandoned the enterprise, even though it was still believed that the Portuguese in general supported him and had kept up secret correspondence with him and supplying him with food for the troops and money, and there was a story that they had even attempted the assassination of the Count de Fuentes with an arquebus. It was thought that if the count had retired into the castle as some had advised him to do, then the city would in fact have risen in favour of Don Antonio.

On receipt of letters from the queen, brought by a ship with stores from England, Drake and Norris wrote to Elizabeth on the 15th, that they had decided to go to San Miguel in the Azores; and then, for the first time, they confessed that Essex was with them. They had met him, they said, to their great surprise, off Cape Finisterre, but could not send him home before, as they could not spare the *Swiftsure* but there was still no word about Sir Roger Williams.

Essex started for England on the 16th of June, two days after his brother. Sir Roger Williams, who was after all with them, want to accompany him, but Drake and Norris refused to let him go, assuming that the presence of Essex might have a mollifying influence on Her Majesty during the weeks before they arrived in England. Also on the 16th Don Antonio wrote to Walsingham in a depressed state of mind that he was receiving daily reports from those returning of the deplorable state of his affairs the result of his misfortune and his sins.

The intention now was that part of the fleet should go to the Azores under Drake, while the remainder under Norris would return with the sick and wounded to England. By the 17th the fleet had not yet set sail due to bad weather.

The governor of Castile arrived with twelve galleys and 2,000 men, but he could not cross the sand bar at the mouth of the Tagus on the 13th owing to the bad weather. It was thought certain that it was his arrival that caused the English to withdraw. With Don Alonzo de Batan and another twelve galleys he went out to chase and harass the English fleet which was lying becalmed, but a breeze got up which allowed them to draw off into the open sea. The Spanish then returned to Cascais in case Drake returned to attack the town even though they had seen him pass Cape Finisterre.

Meanwhile in Lisbon, the raising of the siege had taken the defenders by surprise. They fully believed it to be an attempt to draw the Spanish troops out of the town in order to that the inhabitants might rise and massacre the few Spaniards left. So certain were they of this that an unfortunate Portuguese noble, Count Redondo, who arrived that day and went to pay his respects to the Archduke, was immediately seized and beheaded *"pour encourager les autres."* As soon as the Spanish realised that the English had really gone, Count de Fuentes with his six or seven thousand men again made a reconnaissance, almost to the English position at Cascais, but finding the invaders well entrenched with the fleet behind them, decided that it would be too risky to attack them, and so returned to Lisbon.

News of the Spaniards was brought to the English by some friars, a number of whom always hung about Don Antonio's quarters, and Norris and Essex each promised the messengers a hundred crowns of they found the enemy in the place as reported, because they were spoiling for a fight in the open before they finally embarked. But De Fuentes had already gone back to Lisbon, so the friars lost their reward.

Norris, however, still eager, and sent a page who spoke French, and a trumpeter, post-haste to Lisbon, with a challenge to Fuentes and his army to come into the open and fight. The opportunity was too good for Essex to miss, so he too sent a cartel by the page on his own account, giving every one the lie in a general way and offering to fight anybody in single combat. The messenger came back again without an answer, only that the Spaniards had threatened to hang him for bringing them such insolent nonsense. The Spanish told the story a different way, less honourably for Essex. They said that while the messengers were being entertained "as if they were great gentlemen" at breakfast by some of the captains who spoke French, the letters, which the messengers had said could only be opened with the Archduke's permission, were surreptitiously steamed, read, and re-sealed, and handed back again as if unopened, with the reply that his Highness would not allow them to be opened. So Norris and Essex had their bravado for nothing, and went without their fight.

In Lisbon the people were supposedly as disturbed as ever, feeling that their chance of freedom was slipping away from them, and constantly raised alarms that the English were returning. But the Spanish reinforcements were arriving. When the Duke of Braganza, head of the Portuguese nobility, arrived in royal state with a great body of retainers to help the Archduke, all hope for Don Antonio disappeared.

If Drake could not or would not burn the Spanish fleet on this occasion, he was always a great hand at plundering merchantmen, during the six days that his fleet lay off Cascais he scoured the sea for miles round in search of prizes, taking as many as forty merchant ships coming from Flanders loaded with grain and provisions for Spain and elsewhere and that he intended to sail to the Azores after all, where he could lay his hands on the munitions there. Men from the Dutch flyboats were transhipped into the prizes and the Dutch captains sent off without being paid their freights, and probably glad to get away on any terms.

Lisbon was gradually settling down. People who had been hiding in churches and cellars for the last ten days crept out, possibly under the impression that the Spaniards had all been murdered, and that King Antonio had come into his own again. Their disappointment can only be imagined when they discovered that no one of all the city had dared to strike the blow that would have made Portugal free again. So they patiently reconciled themselves once more to the occupation and cheered his highness the Archduke as he went in state to the cathedral to hear a solemn *Te Deum* of victory.

The Spanish did their best to follow the enemy. Ships in the Tagus were fitted out to watch Cascais and sail after the English fleet, to do all the damage they could, while Don Pedro de Guzman was sent to cut off the English garrison of 400 men at Peniche, who held on until they heard that de Guzman and Sancho Brava were on their way and only then they took to their boats, or at least as many as could do so. De Guzman and his troops urged on their horses until they were ready to drop, but arrived too late to stop the embarkation, except for about 200 men, who were put to death.

The Return

The Spanish overestimated the strength and capability of the English, believing that their Armada would sail from Portugal to take possession of the Azores, which were poorly defended; either that or it would lie in wait to attack the fleet from India which was due to arrive, it being that time of year. But King Philip had moved on and was now concentrating his attention on the turmoil in France, where King Henry, Don Antonio's strongest supporter after Catherine the Queen Mother, had been assassinated and Henry of Navarre was about to convert to Catholicism to become Henry IV of France.

However, the attack on the Azores, the third target on the list from Queen Elizabeth, had been abandoned in view of the rising death-toll among the men on board the fleet and the dwindling stock of victuals.

Independently of the English Armada, a private venture commanded by George Clifford, third Earl of Cumberland, set sail on 18th of June and reached the Azores where they attacked Spanish and Portuguese ships taking prizes, but this was the only English success of the time.

After the English had embarked on the 14th July they hung about the waters off Portugal for four days in an attempt to take at least some booty and provisions. On the 18th they sailed south, taking with them the German barques and fifty French ships that they had captured, laden with wheat, rye flour, cheese, meal, etc., which would be used to supply the fleet. The Spanish thought that if the English reached the Azores they would probably make the wheat into biscuits on one of the islands. The fleet cruised towards Cape Espichel, twenty miles south of the estuary of the River Tagus, making it uncertain for the Spanish to know its destination, whether it was the Azores, as thought most likely, or to Cape St. Vincent, the south western most tip of Portugal, with the intention of entering Cadiz and setting fire to the shipping there and sacking the town. There was also fear for the ships coming from Portuguese India, but then it was heard that they had taken course to another port.

They were seriously afraid that Cadiz was the destination and so the governor of Castile, in nine of "his best ships", followed up the English about 140km/90 miles out to sea, and by closing up to them he was able to do a lot of damage, sinking five ships and capturing eight, killing 600 men and taking 150 prisoners.

Nevertheless it was still thought likely that Drake would sail on towards the Straits of Gibraltar, where, with the anticipated help of the 30,000 cavalry to be furnished by Al Mansur, he would make a landing and attempt to enter Portugal by another way. But of course that help was never to come.

In Lisbon the Spanish were restoring order and punishing the guilty. Philip sent the Duke of Alva, his illegitimate son, to Portugal where he executed more Spanish than Portuguese for their lack of support. The commander who had surrendered the castle of Cascais was beheaded as a warning to others, and his garrison was decimated, forty being hung "as they deserved."

The weather was unfavourable for a voyage to the Azores as intended and the reinforcements of men and provisions sent by Elizabeth were caught in a great storm, so thirty of them took shelter in La Rochelle, but it was all too late to be of any use.

According to English accounts, after the fleet set sail on the 18th of June, it was pursued and harassed by the Spanish galleys from Lisbon that were able to be rowed effectively in a nearly dead calm, three ships were taken or sunk and one burned by her captain, Minshaw, after a desperate resistance. When the wind sprang up, however, the galleys were left behind, but soon the fleet got scattered, men died from scurvy, starvation, and wounds at the rate of a hundred every a day, and were thrown overboard by the hundred. A few Portuguese gentlemen escaped on a Breton ship to Bayonne.

Notwithstanding all this, after ostensibly setting off for the Azores, Drake turned back again and, picking up twenty-five of his ships which had been separated from him, sailed north up the Portuguese coast, taking some prizes. He landed at Oporto to take on water but did no damage. By this time he had only 2,000 men fit enough to fight.

He attacked Vigo but finding it deserted the troops burnt and wasted the town and all the villages around. They defiled churches, knocked down statues, shot at statues and robbed the vestries. "A verie pleasant and riche valley but wee burnt it all, houses and corne, so as the countrey was spoyled seven or eight miles in length," recalled one participant.

As well as burning Vigo, Drake was reported to have gone with fifty ships to find the Indies fleet. Ironically, as he sailed north and then east along the north coast of Spain, he passed Santander where preparations were being made for another Armada.

It was then decided that Drake should to go to Bayonne, to collect the fittest of the men and stores to put on twenty of the best ships to take to the Azores, while the rest of the fleet was to return to England. But for some reason he broke the agreement and passed Bayonne without even calling in, and the thirty ships that were waiting there for him were left to their fate. "Beset with tempest and pestilence," without a commander, the captains decided to make the best of their way to England, in terrible distress due to the lack of provisions and water.

After a ten-day voyage across the notorious Bay of Biscay and up the Channel, the remnants of the fleet arrived at Plymouth on the 2nd of July to find that Drake had already arrived, having abandoned the thought of going to the Azores. On their own initiative, some of the ships of the fleet had gone into other ports so that they could sell their prizes without having to share the proceeds.

The soldiers who arrived in Plymouth with the fleet, those who had survived the sickness and were able, were sent home with five shillings each for their wages, along with their arms. One English chronicler thought it was "verie good pay, considering they were victualled all the time." But this was not the opinion of the men themselves, who had not been allowed to loot in Portugal as much as they thought they had been promised when they enlisted. They said that if they had been permitted to march as they would normally have done through an enemy's country, they would have come back the richest army that ever returned to England.

On board the returning ships, men were falling prey to disease like nine-pins. The seamen, who were unruly by nature, lived a hard life on board at the best of times. The disease afflicting the fleet was probably scurvy, due to a generally poor diet, a lack of fresh food, and tainted drinking water. The cramped, overcrowded, insanitary, badly ventilated, generally unhealthy living conditions, together with the poor food almost literally thrown in, not to mention vermin, provided a breeding ground for contagion.

Then again, Wingfield/Pricket believed that in preparing for the expedition the recruits had been only "The scum of the towns, the sweepings of the jails, were pressed for the voyage," and laid most of the blame for the failure on the kind of men that comprised the soldiery and mariners. He complained that the recruiting justices and mayors of the towns in England were responsible for the "base disordered persons sent unto us as living at home without rule." He claimed that many idle young men, having seen their friends come back after a few months in the Netherlands full of stories about their brave deeds and tales of war, "thought to follow so good an example and to spend like time amongst us," had found the expedition was not the voyage for riches and heroism that they had bargained for, so in their disillusionment they were not likely to make good troops in the field.

Not more than 5,000 of them ever came home and their story was so dismal that "all England rang with reprobation of the bad management and parsimony that had brought the expedition to so inglorious a conclusion".

Drake had arrived with Don Antonio and about thirty of his men in Plymouth on the 10th of July with twenty or thirty ships, with more ships coming in until the 13th, when the remainder arrived with Don Antonio's son, Don Manuel, and John Norris. There were not 2,000 men, soldiers and sailors, between the 100 or so ships, in good health. Thomas Fenner wrote to Walsingham that out of his 300 men only three had escaped sickness. 114 had died on his ship alone.

Another example of the virulence of the onboard plague is that Drake had seized a ship from Flanders in the waters off Galicia, put forty of his men on board with orders to follow him, but so malignant was the sickness that thirty-eight of the forty died.

The news from England as it reached Spain was that the fleet had reached Falmouth in a bad plight; that two thirds or more of the men were dead and those left living were seriously ill, while some ships had been lost. Also, that the people were dissatisfied with the result of the expedition and Queen Elizabeth was in difficulties through want of money. But notwithstanding this, Don Antonio had been very kindly received by Elizabeth, even though the English people put much of the blame for failure onto him, they detested him and viewed him as a person doomed to calamity. In the background, the former friends and colleagues, Drake and Norris, were said to be open enemies.

Besides the ships in Plymouth and those that had put into other ports, the number of missing was about thirty, both English and Flemish. It was believed by some that they had sailed to the Azores, and that altogether only two ships had been lost when they were burnt with the Spanish galleys near Lisbon. The loss of men at this time was thought to be over 8,000, including about 900 gentleman and officers, "the best in England." The total loss was estimated to be as many as 11,000 men.

When the Earl of Essex arrived home he immediately sent his brother to Elizabeth to beg her pardon, while he himself waited fifteen miles away from Plymouth for her reply. He did not make any attempt to communicate with Don Antonio.

Norris, on his arrival, wrote to Walsingham that he supposed Drake had already informed him of the return of the fleet. He sent his brother to learn of Her Majesty's pleasure and the wishes of the Court. He also requested permission to sell the goods taken in the hulks to pay the troops and mariners. He feared that Elizabeth would "mislike" the result of the expedition, but, in an attempt to put a gloss on the event, he said everything had been done with the aim of her majesty's honour, and had the Spanish done as much against England they would have made bonfires in most places of Christendom.

The spy 'David' was able to report to Mendoza that, after the arrival of the fleet in such a wretched state, Don Antonio, through little or no fault of his own, was held in no respect whatsoever, with people insulting him to his face, even calling him and the other Portuguese "dogs," and that the Portuguese were even more unpopular than the Spanish. He also was able, for Philip's benefit, to send a list of names of Don Antonio's Portuguese supporters who had been left at Peniche.

Don Antonio had sent Edward Perrin and Merzouk-Rais, the Moroccan ambassador, to Al Mansur to inform him of his failure and not to send to Portugal but to send to England the money that had been promised on the security of his son Don Cristobal. Needless to say the money was not forthcoming.

He was able to pass on one small piece of good news when he wrote to his friend Juan Luis Estabas Ferreira de Gama to inform him that he had brought his wife Donna Maria and their son Francisco with him from Alvelade in Lisbon, that they were on their way to England on a different ship from his own to another port in England. He advised Juan Luis to send correspondence *via* Dr Ruy Lopez, the Jewish Portuguese doctor to Queen Elizabeth, who, unknown to Don Antonio, was another of Philip's informants.

Don Antonio went to the village of Stonehouse near Plymouth, feeling very miserable and ill-treated. His naturally pessimistic nature was given full vent as he wrote to Walsingham admitting that his own sins deserved even greater punishment and begged for his favour with the queen. He recalled a prophesy by an astrologer that a great victory was in store for Philip. He began to give justifications for the actions of the enterprise.

They had had to call in to Coruna due to a shortage of provisions that were in turn due to the haste in which they had set out. At Peniche the strong wines had increased the sickness of the men so that, after the march, by the time they reached Lisbon, the men were more fit to die than to fight. At the city walls there was a shortage of gunpowder and fire match and no artillery suitable for a siege battery. About Drake, he gave him the benefit of the doubt, believing that he had remained at Cascais by order of the queen to control of the gates of Santa Catalina and San Roque. He wrote, "I am in such a state of mind that I cannot talk."

And yet, by now only in his dreams, he still hoped for help from Elizabeth to march into Portugal and then Spain, "in such force that no mischance or human power can make him turn back." He thanked Elizabeth and offered her his services while awaiting her commands and asked her to thank the generals and colonels on his behalf. He wrote more letters to the same effect that month, acknowledging that he found less support in Portugal than he had been led to believe.

Even now he was not entirely dispirited, he did have a plan that, if he was not well-received by Elizabeth, he would leave for France or Hamburg *en route* to Constantinople or Morocco. He still had a caravel, a small, light, fast ship popular in Spain and Portugal at that time, which was being loaded with arms and stores enough for forty people for four months. He had had a promise of aid from Constantinople and the Grand Turk. Still trusting in 'David,' Don Antonio naively told him that if he didn't find him in London, then to go to Constantinople to find him there. He sent letters with 'David' to France saying that in the event of failure with Elizabeth he would offer his service to King Henry.

Drake and Norris were called before the lords to give an account. Although outwardly Elizabeth received them with affection, she was very angry with them both, blaming them for the failure of the enterprise. Officially she wrote to them as commanders, expressing thanks to God and gratitude be expressed to all for their attempts, "colonels, captains and inferior soldiers and mariners, who had also shown as great a valour as ever nation did."

Don Antonio was at Plymouth and Drake shut himself up at his home at Buckland Abbey, neither of them daring to stir for fear of revenge by the soldiers of the fleet, however, there were very few of them left.

In September the discontented surviving soldiers went to London to demand payment but they were refused, so they attempted to start a riot by trying to burn and sack the city. Elizabeth came from Richmond to Greenwich to order their arrest and four were caught and hung. From the gallows, one of them shouted that this was his payment for going to war.

In Conclusion

By February 1590 Don Antonio had seen Elizabeth only twice since his return in July, 'David' reported him as being "very poor, old and broken, and is living in lodgings taken by the month in the house of a Portuguese woman." Dr Lopez had to give him money, even for his clothes.

Even so he managed to revive himself and sustain his hopes. He was having a ship fitted out secretly to take him to Dieppe to negotiate for a ship to take him to capture Brazil with 1,500 to 2,000 soldiers, failing which he would go to Constantinople, when even now the Turkish fleet was supposed to be intending to sail in summer. Whether anyone took these plans seriously was by now doubtful. Mendoza's trusted 'David' attempted to thwart this plan but he failed and he was at last—much too late—uncovered as the spy Andrada and arrested. Don Antonio had attempted to have 'David' killed, just as 'David' had attempted with Don Antonio by Philip's orders. But when Don Antonio left Plymouth for London he was followed by yet another Spanish spy, 'Marcus', who took Andrada/David's place.

March 1590 saw Don Antonio in a very different frame of mind, the uplifting fantasy of Brazil had dissipated and he was once again in "a miserable condition." Elizabeth was angry with him, as well as Drake, she no longer had reason to rely on Don Antonio, at first she gave him no pension and then only £100 per month, and that with "a very ill grace" because she knew that he spoke badly of her and only wanted to escape from England. He was living in London, "not merely without any magnificence, but in poverty and dejection, as some sailors, who saw him, affirm." He had dismissed all of his servants because he could not afford to keep them.

In April another fantasy came forward with George Clifford, third Earl of Cumberland, who offered to take Don Antonio to Terceira once more with 4,000 or 5,000 men, and it was said that a fleet was actually being fitted out under the Portuguese flag, but a fantasy is all it was.

Nevertheless, Don Antonio and Elizabeth were both sending spies to Portugal and Spain. A spy acting on behalf of Don Antonio was arrested on 28th of April in Lisbon. He had been to Fez where he had had an audience with Al Mansur, and then came to Portugal to spy on the defences there. He told his inquisitors, falsely, that Queen Elizabeth had 400 ships, 200 of which were ready to put to sea destined for France and then the Azores.

But in the meantime, three of Don Antonio's followers had defected and gone to King Philip to crave his pardon. Edward Perrin went once more to Morocco in April to ask for a subsidy of 200,000 crowns, and probably to offer encouragement to Don Cristobal, now seventeen years old, who was still being kept as a hostage. Rather pathetically, Don Cristobal wrote to Burleigh saying that he was hopeful of an early release, if only Burleigh would only give his support.

In June there was a rumour that Don Antonio and two of his sons were with King Henry, formerly of Navarre, now of France. If this been true it would not have displeased the Spanish, who feared that he might have gone to Constantinople where he could have caused much more trouble, but he did indeed send a letter to Sultan Murad III, from where, later in the year, came a report that the sultan would aid a rising in Portugal and requested a son of Don Antonio, who was only twelve or fourteen years old (there two other sons, Dennis and Juan), be put with the Turkish fleet. Al Mansur was to be requested to release Don Cristobal.

In Portugal, even though Spanish opinion was that the city of Lisbon, and therefore the whole country, had been saved for Spain by the English wasting their time at Coruna, so allowing time for preventative measures to be put in place, Philip ordered more troops and cavalry to go to 'support' Portugal, in other words to occupy it more effectively.

The English Armada set sail with three clear instructions from Queen Elizabeth:

1. To distress the King of Spain's ships.
2. To gain possession of at least some of the islands of the Azores in order to intercept Spanish ships to and from East and West indies.
3. To assist King Don Antonio to recover the Kingdom of Portugal if the public were in favour of him.

The first and second objects of the expedition had never even been attempted, while the third object, had it succeeded, would have made Don Antonio, as King Antony I of Portugal, practically a vassal of England.

The taking of Portugal could have been achieved if only the commanders had planned and cooperated better, and if the Portuguese in Lisbon "had not been an utterly terrified set of poltroons," as Wingfield/Pricket called them. On several occasions in Lisbon, when Count de Fuentes and his troops were outside, a witness believed that a few dozen daring men might have seized the gates to turn the tide in Don Antonio's favour.

What was the fate of the central characters? Robert Devereux, Earl of Essex redeemed himself years later in 1596 when, as second in command to Lord Howard, they attacked Cadiz, destroying Spain's naval arsenal and a large part of her fleet. But he fell afoul of Elizabeth and was beheaded for high treason in 1601. Sir John Norris went to assist the new King Henry IV of France in his struggle against the Catholic League, he died in 1597. Sir Francis Drake was in disgrace, it was to be five years before got his next, and last, active command to the West Indies, where he died in 1596.

As for Don Antonio, instigator, participant, and witness in international events of the 1580s, honoured guest but at times plaything and stooge to the court of Queen Elizabeth, the would-be rightful king of Portugal, he finally faced reality and gave up his fight. He went to France where he was given a pension by King Henry IV and died in Paris on 26th August 1595.

The debacle of the English Armada restored the confidence of Spain in its own abilities. In England it had been a failure almost as disastrous as that of the Spanish Armada. In the Spanish Armada, out of 130 ships that set out on 22nd July with 8,000 seamen and 20,000 soldiers, only 53 of the larger ships returned to Spain. 63 ships and 9,000 men were lost.

The English Armada had ruined a good many reputations, including that of its admiral and national hero, Sir Francis Drake. Instead of huge profits from plunder it cost the country £60,000, possibly £16,000,000 in today's money. It had cost the lives, mostly through disease, of as many as 11,000 men out of the 23,000 that had set sail.

Queen Elizabeth ordered that there should be no more discussion about the expedition and a veil was drawn over it. If mentioned at all, the English Armada was modestly referred to as 'The Lisbon Expedition,' a footnote in the history of England.

A 100 Escudos coin of Portugal commemorating Don Antonio